HR: Funny Side Up

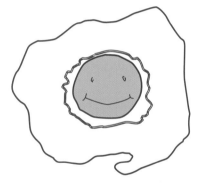

By Elliott Witkin

IHRIM
International
Association for
Human Resource
Information Management

Learning has no limits.

HR: Funny Side Up

Illustrations by
David Clemons
Timothy Jones

An IHRIM Press Book
Published by Rector-Duncan, Inc.
314 Highland Mall Blvd., Suite 510
Austin, Texas 78752 USA

ISBN 9679239-6-4 US$39.00

In memory of Sadie Witkin and Jerome Trier, two terrific grandparents

THE FRONT PAGE

The literary classic *One Fish Two Fish Red Fish Blue Fish*, by Dr. Seuss, ends with a very wise observation:

Every day,
from here to there,
funny things are everywhere.

And that's good to remember, because we spend many of those "every days" at work, where "funny" doesn't seem to be everywhere. Work is serious stuff — we have customers to please, numbers to meet, and budgets to live within. At times, it seems as if laughter has left the building and would not be welcomed back.

Fortunately, that's not the way it is. Dr. Seuss was right — funny things *are* everywhere, just hanging around waiting to be noticed. Over the last 10 years, "The Back Page" column in *IHRIM.link* (and its predecessor, *The Review*) has attempted to search them out, and to present them to its readers for their enjoyment.

This book, a compilation of those columns starting with the first pre-Back Page in 1992 (with the addition of a snappy intro-duction for each one), is a trip through time. It illustrates how technology in general, and the human resource management systems (HRMS) profession in particular, have changed. In editing the columns for this book, I left the technology aspects as they were in the original. Especially in the earlier columns, references that were serious at the time are funny now, like some of the things we said in earnest as teenagers ("when I'm a parent, I'll never make my kids do homework").

We have seen such significant change during this time period that it sometimes seems like today is disconnected from yesterday. It's as if the early and mid-90s were the HRMS Stone Age, when the available tools were so primitive that if you wanted to communicate with the person in the next cube, you had to actually speak with them instead of using e-mail.

Although things were very different "back then," I think having an understanding of the past helps us to realize how we arrived at where we are today. And that's important, not only because of what has changed, but also because of what hasn't changed — that the end users of technology, in whatever its current form, are people. And when you get people and technology together, the outcome has always been fascinating, unpredictable, and often funny (although sometimes it's not as funny to those using the fascinating, unpredictable technology).

HR: FUNNY SIDE UP

In the human resource systems profession, we are very fortunate that our work is so focused on people. In addition to their many work-related talents, everyone we work with has the ability to make us laugh (although sometimes it's polite to wait until they leave to start laughing).

I think it says a lot about the HRMS profession that a column like "The Back Page" could last for so long. After all, it's certainly not in the class of literature with novels such as *Great Expectations*, *Paradise Lost*, and *Beowulf* (that class being works that are assigned to appreciative high school students, who are so eager to start reading that they run right out and buy the Cliffs Notes).

Even though high school students may have missed "The Back Page," you, the readers, have supported the column over the years, and I thank you. In a way, we were all in this together, because it could not have lasted so long without you.

I would also like to thank the many people on the IHRIM board and the Magazine Editorial Committee during this period. Each year when they discussed the magazine content for the upcoming year, they allowed the column to be one of the "keepers."

A special "thank you" goes to the editors of "The Back Page."

Jeannette Brown named it, developed the format, and nurtured it through the early years with some very helpful suggestions. Then Linda Hinkle took over, and she was a strong supporter of the column. And now there's Tom Faulkner, who has the ability to make a writer feel good about his work. Tom's support and enthusiasm were major factors in getting this book published, and I will always be grateful to him.

The final "thank you" is saved for my customers, both in my practitioner and vendor positions. You have allowed me to have a successful career by letting me help you meet your human resource information needs. And along the way, you have helped me to see that work can be fun, and provided me with experiences that let me communicate that fun in a positive way to others. I have been fortunate to work with many talented people who have rewarded me with their kindness, and by sharing the wisdom of their collective knowledge.

Now, as Drew Carey says at the beginning of the show *Whose Line Is It, Anyway?* —

"Come on down, let's have some fun."

WHO DUNNIT?

December 1992/January 1993

This hard-hitting "police blotter" story was the forerunner of "The Back Page." I know it's dated, but that's something I have always wanted said about me, since it wasn't true in high school. Maybe it would sound more current if the characters in this column had their own Web site, which would be located at drag.net.

This is the company, Wally's Widgets, in Los Angeles, California. During the year, the company's employees produce thousands of reports, printed on millions of pages. Usually these reports contain correct information. Sometimes they don't. That's where I come in. I carry an auditor's pad.

It was Wednesday, March 3rd. I was working the day shift in the employee information section. The boss is vice president of auditing, Bruce Wilson. My partner is Jill Cannon. My name is Tuesday.

It was 10:33, almost two hours before lunch. Jill was ready to bite into a huge pickle and sausage sandwich when the phone rang.

The caller was Susan Johnson, an HR administrator in the human resource information center. She'd just been faxed two reports by her vice president. Each report showed a different number of employees working for the company. Johnson needed to come up with an explanation fast.

10:41 a.m. We arrived at her office, located on the company's well-maintained top floor. She invited us in.

"Hello, auditors," she said. "Thanks for coming so fast." She was speaking very quickly. I could tell she was nervous.

"What a terrible thing to happen. I get this fax with two reports — one of which I've never seen before — and I'm supposed to explain the differences. I don't even know where to start."

"We'd like to ask you a few questions," I said. "First, let's take the report you produced. What is it supposed to show?"

"It's a count of all the company's employees," she said.

"Where did it come from?"

"I printed it from the company's HRIS."

"Does it include people on leave?"

"No."

"How about part-timers?"

"They're included."

"What about temporary employees?"

"They're not in," she said, starting to calm down.

"Now Ms. Johnson, can you think of anything else that could explain the differences between these reports?"

"Well auditor, there is one more thing."

"What's that, Ma'am?"

"The timing could be different. Mine is run on a payroll cycle basis, and I don't include future transactions. I don't know what the timing is on the other report."

"That's what we'll have to find out."

"Auditor, is there anything I can give you to help in your investigation?"

"We'll need the two reports so we can check out the other one."

"I also have a lot of documentation I could give you, if you'd like."

"Just the fax, Ma'am."

"I'm really in a spot," she said. "I have to explain these differences, and I think my report is right."

"That's the tough part of this."

"What's that?" she said.

"The other person thinks he's right, too."

Our next step was to find out about the other report. Based on information in the report heading, we were able to track it down to Bob Smith in the budgeting department.

We called Smith to arrange a meeting. He said to come right over.

11:23 a.m. We found Smith's office. It was in a run-down part of the building.

"Mr. Smith," I said. "I'm Auditor Tuesday. This is Auditor Cannon. We're here to investigate a report that we think you produced. We'd like to ask you a few questions."

"Sure, go ahead. I have nothing to hide."

I showed him the report. "Did you produce this?"

"Yes, I did."

"What is it supposed to show?"

"It's a count of all the company's employees."

"Where did it come from?" I asked.

"I have my own system called GIGO. It stands for General Information Generated Online."

"Does it include employee information?"

"Yes, it does."

"What's the source of that information?"

"I get it from budget reports from different departments. Then I put it into GIGO."

"Is there any validation on the input?"

"No, I don't need it. I'm keying from computer reports."

"Do you ever try to reconcile your information with the company's HRIS?"

"No. The HRIS is always behind, and I keep GIGO up to date. In fact, I have lots of friends throughout the company who call me with updates."

Just then Smith's phone rang. "Excuse me," he said. "It's probably another update. Do you mind if I take this call?"

"Go right ahead."

While Smith was on the phone, Jill and I had a chance to talk. "This guy is something," I said. "First, he has his own system. Second, he doesn't have any validation. And third, he never reconciles his information with the company's HRIS."

"Three dumb mistakes," said Jill.

"That's right," I said. "He's dum de dum dum."

When Smith got off the phone, we gave him the bad news. "We're taking you in on a 406 — developing and maintaining a bootleg HRIS. These are your rights. You have the right to remain silent. Anything you say can be used against you in an audit report. You have the right to be represented by your boss. If he isn't present or decides that he doesn't want to touch this one, I don't blame him. Do you understand these rights?"

"Yes, Auditor."

"Is there anything you want to say?"

"I was just doing my job."

"I'm sure you were," I said, "but so were the people who were doing it right."

Dum de Dum Dum

Announcer: The story you have just read is true. The names were changed to protect the innocent. On March 11th, an audit report was issued. In a moment, the results of that report.

Cut to a commercial. An HR professional is buried under a mound of paper. Just as he's ready to give up, Super PC comes flying across the screen. He sits on the desk, blows all the paper away, and hands a diskette to the relieved employee.

Announcer returns: The suspect was found guilty on two counts — one for developing and maintaining his system, the other for causing problems for an innocent, hard-working, really nice HR person. Conviction of these offenses calls for a terrible punishment.

Screen crawl: Smith is now serving his sentence, where he has to verify every field for every employee in the corporate HRIS back to a source document.

HRSP – The Next Generation

June/July 1994

It's fun to speculate on what profession your children will choose. The good news for me is that my daughter's level of interest in following in my professional footsteps has not diminished in the 11 years since this article was written. The bad news is that level is not even as high as a Minnesota cornfield in winter.

When I was a kid, I was sure that I was going to be a professional baseball player. I had all the physical tools, which is still obvious when you see me (I am a hulking 5' 4" and 130 pounds). I worked at it constantly, even to the point of neglecting the development of my human resource systems professional skills. In fact, I have to admit (and I'm a little embarrassed by this) that I spent almost no time preparing for my eventual profession. Of course, now I could kick myself for such short-sightedness. But I was young and didn't know better, and there's nothing I can do about it now anyway.

To make sure that my children don't make the same stupid mistake, I'm already trying to figure out what they'll be when they grow up. Tommy, who's two, will probably be either a human wrecking ball or a CEO. It could still go either way. It'll all depend on if he gets in with the wrong crowd at pre-school that fosters his destructive tendencies and sends him down the CEO path.

With Katie, our five-year-old, it's already obvious what she's going to do. She'll be a human resource systems professional. She has all the signs.

Once, I asked my wife how many children there were in Katie's pre-school class. Before her mother could answer, Katie told us there were 15. It was her first head count report. I didn't ask her if it included part-timers and temporaries. After all,

she was only three.

One night, at the age of four, Katie logged on to our PC, brought up DisplayWrite, created a report, and printed enough copies for distribution to all her classmates the next day. It was a typical human resources report, containing the names of all the people in a unit along with demographic information. At the risk of violating the confidentiality of the information on the report, this is what it looked like:

katiemommydaddytommyjkdklfdskjfiejdlksjfjklsljfkdsjfkslkjfkdjlsjfjfkjfdkjfiefhjehjdksdjfkjkdjfkdjfkdjfdjfdkljfkdkjfkdjf

It was clearer than a lot of reports I've seen. As an enhancement, I suggested that next time she display the descriptions along with the codes.

She already has the concept of having a unique key for each record. She owns more stuffed animals than exist in most countries, and each one has a name. Pinky, Mr. Snuggles, Puffy and Medium Bear, among many others, have a home in her little world. I know it's just a matter of time before she decides to develop an Animal Resource Management System (ARMS). It seems like a good candidate for FoxPro.

My future HRSP'er has already developed the knack of matching a candidate's skills with an opportunity. When she saw a truck that was carrying cars to a new car dealer, she asked how the cars were going to get off the truck. I told her that someone puts on a crash helmet and backs the cars down a ramp, but that you'd have to be crazy to do it. Sensing a perfect match for her little brother's strengths, she suggested that we see if Tommy wanted to do it.

I can see she's got the people skills, but what about data management? No problem there either. One day I saw her going through all her clothes, and I couldn't figure out what she was doing. After a few minutes, she told me she'd been counting them — 12 shirts, seven shorts, six pajamas, 5 million pairs of Little Mermaid panties.

She seems to have all the important qualities, and I would certainly never interfere with her choice of a profession. But I am her father, and if she asks about becoming a human resource systems professional, I'll be honest and tell her that she might want to consider a field where it's easier to keep up with new developments. Like maybe nuclear medicine.

PRESS 6843648 IF YOU WANT TO...

August/September 1994

When this column was written, voice response systems were becoming common. Some were good, and some made you wish that Alexander Graham Bell had gone into another line of work. There has been a great improvement since then, and I'd like to think this column's 10 million readers made some contribution to that.

Voice response systems in human resources are like birth control devices. When used properly, everyone's happy. When used improperly, surprising results occur.

Sure, some companies will use voice response to provide both better and cheaper service to their employees. It's a technology with many known, and some still unknown, benefits. But you can be just as certain that someone, somewhere, will put in the *voice response system from that really hot place where people go in the end* (and I don't mean Miami).

Let's call that company now to find out some information, like maybe the policy for adding a new medical dependent.

We dial the number. It's a 976 number, so don't make a mistake. You could get "Party Talk," only US$49.95 for the first three minutes.

After 12 rings, the call is answered.

"Yo," says a voice as friendly as a collection agent. It is one of those voices that makes you wish for nails on a blackboard, but it's there because the CEO's mailman's son worked cheap.

"You've reached the Benefits Center," it continues. "You's can do lots of things as long as you got a phone with buttons. You can't if you don't. Just remember to enter 34289 after everything. Now, enter your secret number."

We enter our 14-digit PIN.

"You forgot to press the pound sign first. Do it again."

We re-enter our number, this time adding in the key whose purpose is known only to the script writer.

"One more time."

We comply. It has taken us only five minutes to get in.

"Press two for general benefits information. Press 15 for specific benefits information. Press four for individual benefits information. Press 11 for benefit plans information. Press 106 for benefit policies. Press star twice for additional options. Press 39 if you absolutely have to speak to someone. To repeat this menu, hang up and call again."

We take a guess that we want the benefit policies option. Luckily, we remember that the code is 106, and we enter it.

"Please re-enter your choice, followed by a 7."

We do as we're told.

"For policies set by the government, press four. For policies set by the board of directors, press 16. For Benefits department policies, press 42."

We try the benefits department option, which is intuitively obvious to anyone using the system.

"For recent policies press 14. For older policies press eight. For all others, enter the last 12 letters of your last name. To speak to someone, enter the customer service code."

We decide to take one last shot at it and select the "older policies" option.

"For medical policies, press 14. For dental policies, press ZX. For health plan policies, enter $E=mc^2$. For life insurance policies, enter your social security number. For profit sharing enter the plan year."

This isn't exactly what we had in mind when we made this phone call, but we're hooked, so we guess at the medical policies option.

"For help in this area, enter the code to contact a Benefits Center representative."

Since we don't remember the code required to speak to a person, and we don't know how to go backward in the script, we hang up and call again. This time, we know what we're listening for. Eventually, we get in, hear the option we need to enter to speak to someone, and enter it. We're almost there.

"For voice mail press B. For a beeper press VM."

Not exactly what we wanted, but at least it's different. We select voice mail.

"Thank you for calling the Benefits Center. Your call is very important to us, so please leave your name, phone number, social security number, employee number, work location, time you called and a short message."

We give up, another techno-victim.

But we don't have to go quietly. The next time I find myself on the other end of one of these Martian-designed voice response systems, I'm going to call it with an automated dialer and let them exchange tidbits until one of them says "Enter 5276869 to 'say uncle.'"

Database(ball) and .bat Files

October/November 1994

For anyone who names their daughter after Babe Ruth (he is the name-sake of our daughter Katharine Ruth), there could be no better job than to be associated with a baseball team. I'm hoping this article will open those doors. Even if they ask me to be the dirty towel picker-upper, I would say "how much do I have to pay you to let me do it?"

In searching for innovative uses for human resource management systems, I remembered an acquaintance who's an HRMS manager for a major league baseball team. I figured I'd call him and find out how he uses his system to contribute to our national pastime.

When I reached him on the phone, he said he'd be glad to speak to me, but it had to be off the record. It seems that everyone in the team's front office was nervous about budget cuts since the rumor had started that the owner had his eye on a pitcher who could actually throw strikes every once in a while and there might be a need to free up $82 million to sign him.

Naturally, my journalistic integrity prevents me from revealing my source. In fact, I would go to jail before I'd reveal the team's name. I'll only say that they haven't won a World Series since 1908 and their management has been *tinker*ing for*evers* and they still have no *chance* and they aren't exactly a great cub... I mean club. Don't even try to get any more out of me, because I will invoke my first amendment rights by putting my fingers in my ears, humming really loud and shouting "I can't *heeeeeeeeeeeeeeeeeeeeeeeeear you*" over and over until you take my professionalism seriously. Anyway, this phone call to Wrigley Field is long distance, and since the only expenses I get for this assignment are for interplanetary travel, I better get back to the interview.

Journalist extraordinaire reporting knowledgeably: So Steve... by the way, just for my notes, you spell your last name b-u-c-k-l-e-y, right?

Anonymous Source: That's right.

JERK: Could you tell me the biggest problem you have working for a baseball team? (They taught us this question at the Jethro Bodine School of Journalism, so I always use it to get control of the interview.)

AS: Well, it used to be chewing tobacco on the input forms, but now most of the guys just have their agent-in-charge-of-paperwork do it for them.

JERK: It must be interesting working for a baseball team. What are some of the ways you use the HRMS to help the team?

AS: One thing we're really proud of is our safety program and the way we track it. It's important that our players stay healthy, and we want to know that they're looking after themselves. You probably notice all the players examining themselves a lot. We ask that they do it when the camera's on them, and then we record it in our system.

JERK: I always wondered what they were doing. How about training? Other than their baseball skills, what else do you do?

AS: Training is a big area for us. We've just put together an excellent cliché course, so you should notice a big improvement in that area. Now when the players are speaking to reporters, they'll be able to give it 110 percent and they won't have to take it one cliché at a time.

JERK: There must be some unique aspects to your job. Could you share some of them?

AS: Sure. I guess our payroll is unique. We have a terrible problem with dollar field sizes, and our deductions are a little unusual.

JERK: Like what?

AS: Oh, we have the usual ones, like health insurance and union dues. But we also have agent's fees, surrogate autograph signers, and even tailors.

JERK: Why would a player need a tailor?

AS: One of our guys last year thought his uniform was too baggy. It seems he was the only one who could squeeze into it all by himself, so he wanted it taken in.

JERK: Are you using any leading edge technology?

AS: Well, it's not leading edge, but one innovative thing we're doing is to use the check signer to autograph baseballs. We like to say that now it's signing two things that bounce. Ha! ha! ha! ha! Boy, do we get a good laugh out of that one.

JERK: I can sure see why. Is there anything else you want to tell me? (I smoothly close with my question that always gets at the one really juicy tidbit that my subject is just dying to tell me, and now that he's opened up he's ready to spill his guts).

AS: No.

JERK: (I'm now forced to use my assertive follow-up). Uh...really?

AS: Really. Hey, nice talking to you. And remember, it's off the record.

JERK: Steve, Steve! No problem. My mouth is shut. My lips are sealed. You have my word as a journalist.

And *nothing* is more important to me than my word. Except maybe meeting a deadline; or getting the real story, even if I have to make it up; or getting just the right colors in Windows on my PC. And I mean nothing.

HR: Funny Side Up

SANTA'S REAL HELPER

December 1994/January 1995

The world may never realize its debt to HR systems prac- titioners. Yes, Virginia, there is a Santa Claus, and some- times he needs help. This story, which was a "scoop" at the time, shows that these talented professionals know how to deliver the goods.

It was that year again, the one Santa had been dreading for so long. The 100-year labor contract with the elves was up, and he knew that the negotiations wouldn't be easy.

At least this time he had his HRMS, which he called ELFS (Employees and Little Friends System). He knew he'd be able to get the information he'd need to avoid what happened last time. He was still smarting from that.

In the previous negotiation, the elves had gotten him to agree to a shoe allowance for all the workers. They'd decided they all wanted to wear those sharp models with the bells, and Santa had given in.

What he hadn't realized, however, was the large number of seasonal workers he employed. When he found out the cost for their shoes, he knew he'd made a big mistake, and one with disastrous consequences.

In order to make up for the unexpected expenses, Santa had had to raise the prices he charged the toy companies for his overnight delivery service. This, in turn, caused them to raise their prices, which led to the Great Depression.

Santa met with his HR folks to develop a negotiating strategy. He had his HRMS manager, Janet Phillips, run the reports to give the cost figures. At least this time, he felt he had the information he needed.

At the first session, the elves presented their proposal. They were asking for a four percent annual increase, a cost of living increase, comp time and singing lessons. They wanted the comp time because their personal lives were in such a chaotic state as Christmas approached. The singing lessons were to change the public perception that they all sounded like the Chipmunks.

Santa, like all manufacturing operations, was being squeezed by his suppliers, so he countered with a 2.8 pecent increase and a parking subsidy for the elves' reindeers. After a little back and forth, the participants adjourned to plot their strategy.

Santa gave the union's proposal to Phillips, who ran the reports to cost it out. When Santa saw what it would cost, he knew it was way out of line. After all, four percent plus a COLA, compounded over 100 years, is some pretty hefty change.

Santa was in a bind. He certainly didn't want a strike. Since he had an unmovable deadline, he'd be forced to hire and train replacement workers. The last time that happened had been when the elves walked out, even though they were under contract. The new workers had been pitiful, and Santa had been forced to lower the skill requirements for producing the toys. Fortunately, he was saved by a brilliant idea. He gave all the kids pet rocks, which took no skill to produce, and everyone had been happy. He doubted he could come up with as good and simple an idea again.

Still, he knew he needed to adopt a tough stance. At the next meeting, he told the union that there wasn't much room in management's proposal, and if the elves didn't like it they could go to work for a cookie company. The meeting broke up after only 10 minutes.

The elves had expected this, but they were also not in a strong position. They knew that if they didn't work for Santa, their employment prospects were pretty much limited to Saint Patrick's Day and remakes of Snow White.

As both sides examined each proposal, the main sticking points seemed to be the money and the elves' need to have some personal time during the busy season. Everyone, including Phillips, started working long hours, trying to find some common ground. The HRMS manager kept running reports and developing spreadsheets, looking for just the right combination to avoid disaster.

Finally, just as it looked as if all the kids might be getting Son of Pet Rock, Phillips came up with what she thought would work.

She projected the workforce growth over the life of the contract, factored in the effects of automation, and consulted with actuaries regarding the 300-year life expectancy of elves and the effects of future salary increases on pension obligations.

She presented her figures and ideas to Santa. They included a 3.3 percent annual increase, and to address the elves' demand for some personal time, she proposed instituting flextime. She was able to show how the new program would save Santa money by increasing productivity at no cost, and the elves would see it as a benefit.

At the next meeting, the deal was quickly closed thanks to Phillips' hard work. The elves were able to meet their quota in producing such worthwhile toys as Dragons of Death and Cosmic Ooze. Christmas was saved, and HRMS had once again proved its strategic business value.

A Call from the King

February/March 1995

We all have fantasies. And if we convince ourselves that they can be good for our psychological health, we can justify ~~wasting~~ spending more time thinking about them. Now you will know one of mine.

One day I'm sitting in my office minding everyone else's business when the phone rings. Imagine my surprise when the voice on the other end says "Hey Elliott, this is Dave Barry."

I hesitate for a minute, not believing what I've just heard. It's Dave Barry. *The* Dave Barry, my writing idol. I like to write, but I'm just a scribbler. Now Dave, he's a writer, with a capital "W," maybe two.

I try to act calm, like Pulitzer Prize winners call me every day. "Hello, Mr. Barry, sir, oh scribe of scribes. I really admire your work."

"I feel the same way," he says. "I admire it too."

"To what do I owe the honor of this call, your royal authorness?"

"I'm really jealous of you," he says.

"Me?," I wonder out loud. The great Dave Barry jealous of *me?*

"Yeah," he says. "Jealous of you. I have to write about mundane things like Super Bowls, the Olympics and world leaders. Not only is it boring, it's hard to think of funny stuff about people like politicians. Now you, you lucky stiff, you get to write about fun things like what you do with computers. By the way, what exactly are human remorse systems?"

"Well, actually, Mr. Barry, it's human resource, but that's okay. People make that mistake all the time. Anyway, human resource systems help an organization manage its people."

"Oh, now I get it," he says. "Like those shiny spinner things that executives use to decide whether they should fire or promote someone. I always wondered who gave them those things. Hey, that sounds like a swell job, and a bunch of can't-miss columns."

"Uh, sir, it's a little more complicated than that, although I'm sure that's an important part of it. You see, technology is changing so fast, and it's up to us in this profession to use it to support the business objectives of our organizations."

"Oh yeah, technology. I'm a great believer in using the latest stuff everywhere. Why, I myself have just completed some intensive study in that area, by which I mean that I can finally use my electric toothbrush, and now I can go on to some of the more advanced subjects, like my VCR, which comes with a very simple manual, which (and I am not making this up) explains the bigger manual that up to now I have displayed on my coffee table as an example of fine literature, which I also believe in, unless of course it involves actual reading, in which case I'd watch the movie on my VCR, if I could only figure it out."

"Uh, yeah, OK. Listen, while you're on the phone, is there anything you can suggest to help me become a better writer about human resource systems?"

"I sure can. The most important thing is to know your audience. What is yours like?"

"They're extremely professional, dedicated and well educated," I tell him. "They work hard at their job, but they also like to have a good time."

"With that type of audience, there are three principles you should always follow. First, take the high moral ground on the issues that are most important to them. Second, respect your readers and never write down to them. And third, use the advanced journalistic technique of including the word "sex" in every column."

"Hey, that's a big help. Thank you very much, sir," I said.

"Sure thing. Well, nice talking to you. Maybe one day I'll be lucky enough to get to write about human recourse systems. Now I'm going to hang up if I can just figure out how to use my programmable phone."

An HRMS That Really Is a Scree-um

April/May 1995

New opportunities and situations arise every day, requiring us to develop creative solutions. These groundbreaking new ideas are essential to produce continuous innovation in the HR systems field. Of course, some ideas break more ground than others.

They're creepy and they're kooky,
Mysterious and spooky,
They're altogether ooky,
The Addams fam-i-ly.

We join Morticia and Gomez in their cheery family room:

"Morticia, ha ha, guess what."

"What, Gomez darling?"

"We're broke. Isn't that great?"

"Yes it is, but what are we going to do?"

"I've been doing some reading, and I think we can make a lot of money by developing a human resource management system."

"Oh, Gomez, you're so smart. Do you think we can do it?"

"Of course. Between us, Uncle Fester, Mama, Lurch, Thing and Cousin It, who could ever put together a team like that other than Microsoft?"

"And don't forget Wednesday and Pugsley. They're so adorable, we can use them in our advertising."

"I'll get started right away," Gomez says as he does a backflip into his study.

Gomez labors for several months, spending hours standing on his head while he works through hundreds of issues. One day Morticia pops in to lend some cheer to the effort.

"How is the work going on the database?" she asks.

Gomez puts down his pencil and walks over to her, an excited look on his face. "Cara mia," he says as he kisses Morticia's arm. "I just love it when you talk techie."

Gomez presses on and makes remarkable progress on the project, skillfully blending the unique talents of his team members. He appoints Cousin It director of quality assurance because, as Gomez says, "Cousin It can see ahead to anticipate problems. He never misses a thing."

They finally reach the point where they're ready to enter data into a system prototype. Thing is named as director of data entry and spends many days keying in data. Unfortunately, the project hits a snag when Thing develops Carpal Tunnel Syndrome and has to be put in a full body brace.

Finally the system is ready to show to prospective customers. The first one comes to the door and is greeted by Lurch, director of marketing and sales. Lurch picks up the customer by the back of his jacket, carries him into the study, and drops him in a chair.

"Welcome," says Gomez, a warm smile on his face as he sits down at his PC. "Let me show you the system. I'll start with our training module."

Gomez double clicks and a full-screen picture of Uncle Fester appears, a light bulb glowing brightly in his mouth.

"That's very interesting," says the customer, "but I'm more interested in personnel actions. What can you show me there?"

"No problem," says Gomez. "Let me show you how we do terminations."

He double clicks, and a picture of a large Venus's-flytrap appears. He clicks again and a picture of an employee appears.

"You simply apply the action to the employee," he says as he drags the image of the employee and deposits it on the plant. The plant chews for a few seconds, and when it opens its petals the updated employee record appears.

"Very, uh, unusual," says the customer. "What else do you have to show me?"

Gomez' face lights up. "Here's some special processing related to layoffs," he says. "You just click on this guillotine icon..."

"I think I've seen enough," says the customer as he runs out the door.

Morticia comes in. "How did it go?" she asks.

"I think we've made a sale. He was so impressed he ran off to get a purchase order."

"Gomez, you're brilliant."

They dance the tango across the study, oblivious to everything in the world but each other.

We All Almost Speak the Same Language

June/July 1995

It might seem hard to imagine, but there was a time when tension existed between mainframers and PC types. The relative strengths and (especially) weaknesses of each platform were the topic of many heated discussions, which often ended with participants using technical terms such as "nanny, nanny, boo boo."

Bruce Williams was in a dither. As the Assistant to the Executive Assistant for Issuing Public Meeting Permits, he was the city official in charge of making sure that opposing groups didn't schedule competing rallies. He just realized that he had made the mistake that was the nightmare of everyone in his profession.

In checking the schedule, Williams discovered he had granted a permit for a rally to the BIG MACs (the Association for Big Immense Giant Monstrous Ancient Computers), an organization of mainframe computer supporters. At the same time, right across the street, a similar rally had been approved for a PC organization, the We're Just Gonna Try This And Hope It Works 'Cause It's Never Been Done Before (WJGTTAHIW'CINBDB).

It was just one of those things that happens, and he knew that all he could do now was try to minimize the damage. He decided to do some research.

From what he could gather, the two groups had common goals and dealt with similar issues, but they had difficulty communicating with each other. Information didn't seem to pass easily between them, always requiring an intermediary that never seemed to work just right. Although they had a lot in common, the mainframers and PC'ers rarely saw eye-to-eye on an issue. A confrontation seemed inevitable.

When both sides heard they would be across the street from each other, they stepped up their planning effort. The BIG MACs dusted off the backup contingency disaster recovery plan that they had been working on for 12 years. The WJGTTAHIW'CINBDB'ers decided they'd do whatever they wanted and would just try something else if it wasn't working.

The day of the rallies arrived, and both groups started gathering. It was easy to tell them apart. The mainframers were all dressed in black, with neatly arranged green letters on their shirts, 80 columns across, 24 rows down. The PC'ers were dressed in every color imaginable, with each person looking different. They looked like they were going to a screen saver convention.

It all started innocently enough, with each side holding up signs and chanting slogans. The groups were pretty much ignoring each other.

Then the insults started. The PC'ers began shouting buzzwords and acronyms at the mainframers, who didn't know what hit them. The mainframers threatened to throw their 30-volume requirements manuals at the other side. It was getting ugly.

The police assigned to crowd control were at their wit's end. They just couldn't get the groups to communicate. The officers tried everything they knew, each time thinking they'd finally found the solution, each time getting more frustrated with their failure.

Just as the situation was beginning to look hopeless, a car drove up. Two undercover officers, code name Middleware, got out and asked if they could help.

The new arrivals positioned themselves between the groups, and the noise began to die down. One of the BIG MACs even suggested that he had an application that was ideal for a spreadsheet. A member of the WJGTTAHIW'CINBDB'ers said that she could use some extra processing capacity to handle a very large database.

Slowly, the groups began to mingle until you couldn't tell where one stopped and the other started. After a short meeting (which was attended by 30 BIG MACs and one WJGTTAHIW'CINBDB'er) to determine the appropriate protocol, they all walked off together, arm in arm, down the information superhighway.

The Times They Are A-changing (and A-changing)

August/September 1995

This column takes a trip into what was then the future. Now that we have lived through part of that time, I see there is some truth to the saying that "the future isn't what it used to be."

Anyone who's been in human resource systems for at least a week has realized that the rate of change is accelerating. How many people, though, have really made an effort to study this issue in depth and become an expert? Well, I'm not going to either. I'll just take the easy way and call the future and find out. Since I don't know what it'll cost, I'll call collect.

I dial the number of a large company that makes snack food, because I figure if they aren't around, then life as we know it will have ceased to exist. (For those of you who are concerned that I might actually call the future and run up a really big bill for some poor unsuspecting company, there's no need to worry. I'm not really calling the future. What I'm doing is using an advanced journalistic technique called "lying.") I ask for the HRMS manager, and after a long explanation on my part, the operator realizes that I want the person utilization technology leader. He asks if I want to speak to the person currently in the position, or the one that will take over tomorrow, or the one for the day after that. I ask for the person *du jour*, and get connected.

After introducing myself, I ask what's on this busy manager's agenda. She says that they had implemented a new global-wide system that morning, and that at first, people were happy with it, but after an hour its performance had not improved significantly and they would be replacing it tomorrow.

I tell her I'm impressed with how quickly they can develop things. "It's this new methodology we're using," she says. "It's called S.O.L. Application Development. That stands for speed of light. We were going to use a different methodology, but it was out-of-date by the time we heard about it."

"Can you tell me more about it?" I ask.

"It really works great. By using it, we can develop systems almost instantaneously. Unfortunately, our users view these systems as out-of-date almost immediately."

"How do you deal with that?"

"One way is with new hardware. At the end of each day, we just throw the old computers in the chip bucket and bring in new ones, so we can count on at least a 500 percent improvement in performance each day. It's not much, but every little bit helps."

"Who are the key people on your staff?"

"I have two," she says. "One is the person in charge of acronyms, which is a demanding job when you implement a new system just about every day. The other is my director of change."

"What does that second person do?"

"His job is to make sure that nothing gets out of date. If something hasn't changed in a week, he just changes it however he wants, and he doesn't need a reason. Between you and me, I think he's executive material."

"With things changing so fast, it must be hard to plan," I say.

"Sure it is, but I still need my short-range and long-range plans. For instance, I have a pretty good idea about what I'll do over the next 10 minutes, but the long-range part, like two days or more, gets kind of iffy."

"I don't want to take up any more of your time. You probably could have implemented two systems during our conversation."

"Yes, I do have to go. In a few minutes the data terminator runs and gets rid of any files I haven't looked at since yesterday, so I've got to check that my file-look-at utility ran."

"What does that do?" I ask.

"It opens the files I want to keep just in case. You never know what you might need."

And that's something I doubt will ever change.

Love Letters, Faxes and E-mail

October/November 1995

Nothing is more rewarding for a writer than to hear from readers. Some feedback is positive, and some comes from people who don't know what they're talking about. I have kept all the encouraging notes, and during those times when things look bleak, I re-read both of them.

HR: Funny Side Up

As you would expect, the "The Back Page" generates thousands of letters from admiring readers such as yourself. I make an effort to respond to each one personally by form letter. In the interest of sharing this valuable information with the widest possible audience, here is a representative sample of the notes received.

On the column regarding the Chicago Cubs' use of their HRMS:

Dear obvious White Sox fan:

There was no need to remind us that we haven't won a World Series since 1908. Have you ever stopped to realize that during most of that time the Cubs have had to operate without an HRMS? Don't you think there's a connection there?

The Cubs

Dear Cubs:

You may be right. I bet if you had a good HRMS and Babe Ruth and the rest of the 1927 Yankees, you could probably finish at least fourth in your division.

On the column regarding voice response systems:

Dear person who is resisting progress:

As someone who has successfully implemented a number of voice response systems, I have some very strong comments on your column that made fun of the worst of these systems. Press 6 to learn what I think of you. Press 14 to learn what I think of your abilities as a "writer." Press 852 to learn what I think of your funny looking kids.

An admirer

Dear admirer:

I cannot agree with you that I am resisting progress. To show how open minded I am, I tried pressing 6 but the dial on my rotary phone didn't move.

On the column regarding the role of HRMS in Santa's negotiations with his elves:

Dear snitch:

My labor negotiations are supposed to be confidential. Who leaked?

Santa

Dear Santa:

Rudolph. Check the snow.

On the column regarding my then 5-year-old daughter Katie and her future in HR systems:

Dear Daddy,

Thank you for your concern for my career. My choice of profession is obviously of paramount importance to me. I appreciate your illuminating comments and am eagerly looking forward to developments in that regard.

Love,
Katharine Ruth Witkin, Ph.D., SPHR

My dear Katie,

Huh? Could you please use smaller words?

On the column describing my conversation with my idol, Dave Barry:

Dear Elliott:

Although everyone thinks I have a cushy job, your column points out how hard it is to be funny all the time. I say this because you are trying to do it and — I don't mean this in a bad way — your stuff stinks.

Best regards,
Dave Barry

Dear Dave:

Thank you for noticing my work. It means a lot to me.

On the column regarding the HRMS developed by the Addams family:

Dear colleague:

Since your article about our client/server HRMS, our sales have gone through the roof — or maybe that was Uncle Fester's new invention that went through the roof. Anyway, please stop by to see us. The children are dying to show you the new game they made up with poison darts.

Gomez Addams

Dear Gomez:

Glad to help. I figured if your system was client/server it must be the answer, although I still don't know the question.

On the column regarding the differences between PC's and mainframes:

Dear voter in 1996 and 2000:

Your article on PCs versus mainframes, although exceptionally insightful, thought provoking, and otherwise complete, failed to point out the major difference, as demonstrated by research, between the two hardware platforms. Based on a US$10 million

HR: FUNNY SIDE UP

government study, conducted in my home district, it has been proven, with a 95 percent probability of accuracy, that mainframes come in big boxes and PCs come in little boxes.

Newt Gingrich

Dear Knute:

Thank you for bringing that vital research to our attention. You have made a valuable and cost effective contribution to our knowledge base.

HRMS Gets a Good Rap

December 1995/January 1996

At the time this was written, Shaquille O'Neal played basketball for the Orlando Magic. He has since gone on to achieve modest success with the Los Angeles Lakers and the Miami Heat (modest compared to most of us in the HRMS field). Fortunately for him, this column appeared at just the right time and was the big break in his career.

The negotiations between the Orlando Magic basketball team and Shaquille O'Neal, their petite seven-foot, 300-pound center, were almost complete when they hit a snag. It wasn't over money; US$100 million over 10 years was livable for Shaq. The sticking point was that he wanted the additional visibility of being the spokesman for an HRMS software vendor. Using a little persuasion, such as free tickets and a pair of socks that were actually worn in a game but never actually washed, the team got a vendor to agree.

The marketing campaign is being planned now, and it's supposed to be super-secret (sort of like the actual benefits of client/server), but I happen to know someone at the ad agency. At first he wouldn't tell me about it, so I employed an advanced journalistic technique to obtain the facts, but he wouldn't take a bribe. "No way," he said. "I have my principles." I finally got him to agree to tell me after I promised to do my impression of Godzilla in the movie *Bambi Meets Godzilla*.

For those of you who haven't seen this excellent movie, it starts with Bambi standing serenely in a meadow of wildflowers. For about 30 seconds, we watch cute-as-a-button Bambi gazing at the world and enjoying nature. Then, from the top of the screen, a big foot comes down and squashes Bambi flatter than a floppy disk. The end.

Anyway, I got a chance to look at the ad campaign, and you will not be able to resist running right out and buying not only one, but many copies of this product. I can't tell you any more about the product other than to say that you will never again get a virus, and neither will your computer.

Now to understand how this campaign is centered around Shaquille, you need to know something about him. He is obviously a very large person. He is in fact so large that his information would take up three times the number of records as a normal person in an HR system.

He also perceives himself as a rap star and has actually recorded an album. I haven't heard it, but if he says he's a rap star, then I believe him. I'm not going to write anything negative about his rapping ability, and I certainly wouldn't say anything if I met him face to waist. I wouldn't want to get on his bad side and end up like poor Bambi.

Anyway, one ad that will appear in professional journals has Shaquille slamming a basketball through a basket that is higher than I could reach with a 20-foot ladder. The tag line for this ad is: "What else can I show you about our input process?"

A second print ad shows Shaquille holding a basketball high over his head. The company logo is on the ball, and several people in business suits are jumping up trying to get it. At the top of the page it says: "For quality and service, no one can touch us."

Another ad, destined to become a TV classic, has Shaquille standing in front of a rainbow-colored computer. Rap music is playing, and he starts to dance and rap:

My name's Shaquille
I'm hear to say
This product is great
So buy it today.

It's client server
And re-la-tion-al
It does it all
And that's no bull.

It's double double perfect
You're gonna want two
One for your user
And one for you.

I mean you,
I mean you,
I mean you, you, you, you, you!!!
And when he says you, you get the feeling that he means *you*!!!

COMBATING CONVERSION AVERSION

February/March 1996

If you're ever bored, an interesting way to pass the time is to list all the fun things about doing a data conversion. My list would include: "it's a good way to give the least senior people a feeling of ownership in the project."

Mention the word "conversion," and some HR systems people will have a neutral reaction, such as throwing up. Others, however, will have stronger feelings and view the process as about as much fun as a root canal, but not quite.

I like conversions, but I'm probably in the minority. I've been through several, and the only lasting effect (and I don't consider this significant) is that I used to be six feet tall and I'm now 5' 4".

Of course, conversions aren't simple. They involve taking a huge amount of information, painstakingly accumulated over many years, and translating it into another structure. It's somewhat like the process of creating the "elevator music" version of a Jimi Hendrix song.

And I also have to admit that conversions can use up their share of paper, but normally no more than 50 to 100 boxes. I've sometimes thought that the best way to save trees would be to write a generic HR conversion program to cut down on testing.

Something I like about conversions is that they weed out the real from the fake data. By fake data, I mean the stuff that has been maintained for many years (at great cost), and although everybody knows it's as valuable as the keypunch machine on which it was originally created, everyone's afraid to get rid of it "just in case." For this data, conversion is like cleaning out closets, although conversions, like Halley's Comet, happen more frequently.

Something else I like about conversions is how intimately you become acquainted with your test cases. By the end, you feel as if you know everything there is to know about these people, and you end up wanting to send them birthday cards.

Of course, you have to be willing to enter into the Twilight Zone to do conversions. How else could you explain that it's normal to find people hired before they were born, or terminated before they were hired, or younger than their kids?

You also have to be a detail person. By detail, I mean the type of person who, while watching the Super Bowl on TV, sees a crowd shot from the blimp and says "I really like the earrings that woman is wearing." Based on the checking that has to be done, it also doesn't hurt to choose the "vision option" during that year's benefits open enrollment.

A major decision during conversion is what to do with the interfaces and reports that are using the current data. There are usually two general strategies.

One is to change all the other systems to use the new data in the new format. This is the "change your kitchen cabinets and appliances to match your favorite paper towel holder" option. (Incidentally, my wife and I have used this approach in every house we have bought, and I'm not bragging when I say that the savings on paper towel holders have added up to some pretty hefty change.)

The other option is to take the newly converted information, reconvert it back to its original format, and leave all the existing interfaces alone. This approach can be called the "take apart an airplane, assemble the parts into an automatic transmission, and put it back together" approach.

Whichever you choose, it's a relatively straightforward process, sort of like completing lines 1 through 31 (but not lines 10, 15 and 22) of IRS form 1386, where you figure the amount of depreciable farm equipment purchased in the last 10 years minus nondeductible crop subsidies received from bond-offering federal agencies.

I hope you will now look forward to your next conversion with much more enthusiasm, and don't even think that as you're doing some of the inevitable data transformations, it's an ideal time to slip in a little raise.

Client/Server – A Four-Year-Old Could Understand It

April/May 1996

We now take the existence and the benefits of client/server applications for granted. It's easy to forget that there was a time when the only certainty about them was that they were more complex than quantum physics.

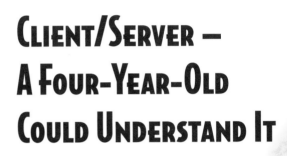

One day I'm sitting around watching my four-year-old son, Tommy, playing, and as usual, I'm thinking of really important things, such as who decided the exact best spacing for the perforations in rolls of toilet paper, when it suddenly hit me. By *it*, I mean one of Tommy's poison darts from his wonderfully educational toy, Legions of Death, whose purpose is to rid the earth of villains which cost US$12.95 apiece.

But something else hit me at the same time, and it was the realization that client/server applications and the play environment of a little kid are so similar that I finally understood where the technical model came from.

Before I explain in great detail why this revelation should have been so obvious, let me first give you a little background.

Client/server, as most people know, was invented by Carl Client and Sally Server, who, like other famous couples such as Rogers and Hammerstein, were married, but not to each other. A lesser known fact was the contribution of Joe /, who got caught in the middle between his two fellow inventors.

With that background (and I apologize if that was such common knowledge that I shouldn't have mentioned it), let me point out the obvious similarities between "C/S" and "C/P" (child's play).

With each of them, you have to put a lot of things together. Now, I'm not exactly a do-it-yourselfer, but I can use basic tools to do simple stuff like screw in a nail with a pair of pliers. But client/server must be really complicated, because PC people always carry these weird toolkits, which are exactly like doctor's instruments except (and I don't think this is a coincidence) they don't contain anything sharp. As I learned at Tommy's last birthday, in addition to being necessary for working on PCs, the tools are also required for putting together kids' toys.

Sample from the instructions for one of Tommy's toys:

To assemble this toy, the only tools required are a hammer, pliers, and one of those little super-teeny screwdrivers you can only find in a PC toolkit.

Another striking similarity between client/server and kids' playing is the distribution of all the stuff involved. For example, Tommy has a huge cabinet for his toys, and by huge I mean he will be able to park his car in it when he's a teenager. But does he put his toys in it? No. He puts them everywhere else, including places normally meant for uses such as baking.

Now consider client/server. There's a big mainframe just waiting to hold all the programs and data and presentation logic, but does anyone put those things there? No. The data sits on a machine in Wisconsin, the programs are on 100 servers in 20 states, and the presentation logic is on 1,000 PCs on four planets.

This arrangement, of course, would make sense to Tommy.

Now if these examples haven't been convincing enough, consider one final similarity. This one relates to the main attribute of little kids' toys, which is that you have to constantly replace them. Even if the toy has been tested for durability by the Marines and examined by child psychologists for its age-specific suitability, it is only a matter of hours before the toy is in pieces, obsolete, or down the toilet.

That quality, of course, is also one of the features of client/server. With all the hardware and software pieces, there is always something needing fixing, which isn't usually necessary, because if it isn't repaired in a few days, there's always a replacement that's better and cheaper.

Now that you can file this information in your directory labeled "indisputable facts," you may wonder what practical value it has. I wondered too, until it (both another dart and the practicality) hit me. I am making Tommy available for consulting on client/server projects. His company will be called 3D, and he will specialize in design, development, and (especially) destruction.

THE THREE CON-STOOGE-ANTS

June/July 1996

Although The Three Stooges "worked" at occupations such as plumbers, detectives, and salesmen, they never tried consulting. That's too bad. I think they would have been successful at it. After all, who wouldn't be able to view a business problem from a fresh perspective, following a pie fight?

The phone rings, and Moe answers it. "Ketchum and Fleesum Consultants," he says. "We fix it even if it ain't broke."

The voice on the other end is frantic. "We have to run our year-end payroll, we're getting tons of errors, our programmer just quit, and all the other consultants are booked. Can you help?"

"We'll be over right away."

Moe yells for Larry and Curly. "Come on, boys," he says. "We've got a live one."

They grab their briefcases and run for the door, all of them trying to get through at the same time.

They ride their bikes to the job and walk into the payroll manager's office.

"Hello-o, hello-o-o, hello-o-o-o," they sing in turn. And then in unison, "Hello."

"I'm so glad to see you," the manager says. "Will this job be in competent hands?"

"Soi-ten-ly," says Curly. "We're always incompetent."

The three of them sit down with the program listings and test results. After a while Curly yells "I can't see! I can't see!"

"What's the matter?" asks Moe.

"I've got my eyes closed."

Moe hits him over the head with a keyboard.

"Oh, look!" says Curly as he points to the shattered keyboard.

"Why, you numbskull!" shouts Moe. "Now look what you've done. You broke the typewriter."

"That isn't a typewriter," says Larry. "It's a calculator."

"What do *you* know, porcupine?" Moe snorts. He tries to cut off Larry's nose with a pair of scissors. "Now both of you get back to work," he orders.

Curly sits at a workstation and makes changes to production programs just to see what they'll do. One of the jobs starts printing on a high-speed printer. He watches as the pages keep coming out, one line on each page. Eventually a whole box of paper is finished. He puts in another box, which also gets used up. After a while the printed paper is stacked about four feet tall, and the report is still printing.

Meanwhile, Larry is busy reviewing test results. "I think I found the problem," he says to Moe. "They're trying to run year-end and today is only December 30th. They have to wait until midnight tomorrow."

"You knucklehead," shouts Moe as he pokes Larry in the eyes. "By then it's too late because it'll be next year."

Meanwhile, Curly is still standing by the printer, where the paper is now over his head. Finally, the printer stops. "Nyuk, nyuk, nyuk," he chuckles. The printer starts up again. "Oh, wiseguy," he says. "I'll show you!" The printer stops. "That's better." It starts again. "Oh, so you want to play rough, do you?" Curly lifts up the cover on the printer and looks in. The cover closes on his head. Curly starts yelling, and Moe comes over.

"Hey melonhead, what're you doing?" he yells. "I thought you were testing."

"I was," says Curly. "But this thing wouldn't stop."

"I'll stop it," says Moe. He pulls out the plug and wraps the cord around Curly's neck. "Now get to work, you lamebrain."

Just then the manager comes by. "How's it going, he asks?"

"We're done," says Moe as he hands him the bill. "All you have to do is wait until 10 minutes after we leave and then run payroll."

"I don't know how to thank you enough," the manager says. "Now I can get these paychecks off to our office in Niagara Falls."

"*Ni-a-gara Falls*," they repeat together, as slowly they turn, step by step, inch by inch, and ride off on their bikes, with *Three Blind Mice* playing in the background.

ON THE ROAD WITH HRMS

August/September 1996

*When it comes to business travel, people can be split into two groups —
those who think it's glamorous, and those who actually travel. My trips
have provided me the opportunity to see many places, some of which were
planned.*

A growing number of people in the HR systems field travel quite a bit. Vendors, consultants or practitioners — at any moment there is more HR systems knowledge waiting at airport luggage carousels than existed in the whole world when we first loved Lucy. Travel can be filled with fun and adventure, and I highly recommend it if you enjoy meeting unusual people, going somewhere you hadn't planned on, and wearing your clothes (including those nobody usually sees) an extra day.

My own bit of fun and adventure begins on one of those days that make the midwest as enjoyable in winter as Siberia, but without the scenery. Following a meeting in Rochester, New York, my itinerary takes me to Detroit and, after a change of planes, home to Champaign, Illinois, a small college town in the middle of nowhere, unless you consider thousands of acres of corn fields to be somewhere. There is a major snowstorm over the midwest, but with any luck I'll be home for dinner.

At the airport in Rochester, I make the first of two big mistakes — I check my suitcase. *Do not ever do this.* Even if you have one of those steamer trunks that can hold an elephant, insist that it will fit under the seat and carry it on the plane.

This leads me to the second, and most critical, mistake I make today — getting on the plane. By itself, this isn't so bad, as the plane from Rochester to Detroit is a "normal" one on an airline whose name you would actually recognize. However, this action ensures that I will later have to get on a plane from Detroit to Champaign, and *that's* where the problems begin.

To understand why, you need to know something about the airlines that serve small towns like Champaign. These are not real airlines. Oh sure, they have so-called planes, but they are airlines in the same sense that shoppers who are being watched on closed-circuit television are TV stars.

On these planes, the "pilot" has only a first name. ("Your pilot today is Captain Bob.") At first I thought this was for informality, but now I think it's more for their protection. I have actually seen one of these pilots walk out to his plane and spin the propeller. This gives new meaning to the term "propeller head."

Returning to the traveling HR systems person, the flight to Detroit is fine, but then I change to Captain Bob's plane. There are, of course, no indoor jetways onto his plane, so today, while it's snowing heavily, everyone just slogs through the slush.

Five minutes before we are supposed to land, Bob announces that the visibility is too poor to land in Champaign and we will be going to, oh, let's say, Minneapolis. Since that's only about 500 miles from where we expected to go, with no chance of getting back tonight, you wouldn't think people would get too upset, but some do.

Unfortunately, this is where the weirdos come out. These are people who take everything they own on the trip, except their brains. One guy starts screaming at Captain Bob, "Why can't you land in Peoria?" (Would *you* land in Peoria?) Another person stands up and says, "OK, I'm going to tell a joke. There was this man and this woman, and they were in the bedroom doing you know what…" He is telling this joke to a group of people that *he doesn't even know*. I am thinking of asking for a parachute so I can jump out, not so much to get home but to get away from these people that I will be trapped with for another two hours.

Trying to make the best of a bad situation, and knowing I have a client in Minneapolis, I decide that I will meet with them tomorrow and go home that night, probably with Captain Kangaroo.

We land in Minneapolis around 5:30, and I try to get my suitcase. After four and a half hours at the airport, I find out it is still in Detroit and will be cheerfully sent to Champaign in the morning. OK, so no clothes for tomorrow.

After only an hour wait for a cab, I get to my hotel room. There is a USA Today outside it, but since it is almost midnight, it is more like USA *yesterday*. I find the prediction of today's weather particularly interesting. Unpacking takes literally no time.

I will now pass along a little traveling hint. If you wash certain items of your clothes in the sink (and I'll only mention this in brief) and let them dry overnight, some of them get very stiff.

The next day I meet with my clients, but being in yesterday's clothes, I keep my distance from them. Captain Hook brings me home, and I am ready to embark on another exciting adventure in the high-flying world of HR systems. Although next time I'll walk from Detroit to Champaign — it's much faster.

The Internet and You...and Everyone Else

October/November 1996

Several years ago, on my performance review I listed that one of my professional development goals for the upcoming year was to "Become more proficient in using the Internet." At the time, it was appropriate to devote special attention to learning to use that technology in our daily work. Today, if someone wrote it as an objective, it would sound like: "In the upcoming year, I plan to diligently apply myself to learning more about using a pencil sharpener."

It is now impossible to go more than 10 minutes without hearing about the Internet, even if you're underwater. At a fast food place, they ask if you want a Web site with your burger. On the Weather Channel, they now tell you the winds are .com. Even my kids send e-mail to my wife and me to tell us that, no matter what's planned for dinner, it sounds yucky.

The Internet even has its own symbols. Many people know that :-) stands for a smile and :-D signifies laughing out loud. Less well known is that % means percent, and # is the symbol for let's play tic tac toe.

Since the Net is everywhere, as a public service I'll assume my alter ego of Browser Bob and answer some FAQs (that's cyber talk that means "For A Quarter") on this topic.

What is the Internet?

"Internet" comes from the Latin word "Internet," which means many connected nets. But don't be fooled by this simplistic explanation, because the Internet is actually many, many connected nets.

Who started the World Wide Web?

Spiderman.

Who pays for the Internet?

The federal government. I have been billing them for years and they have always paid. They must feel it's a good investment in the country's technological infrastructure, plus there's probably someone who feels extremely important to be responsible for paying the Internet bill.

Just so I can avoid them, what are the addresses of the adults only Web sites?

I can't answer that, because my children read this magazine. (I bribe them, including Tommy, who's in pre-school, to read my column and laugh at it :-D.)

What do all those letters mean in Web site addresses?

please/dont-ask.me-such/hard.questions.@i.dont.know.com

How can the Internet help me in my job?

The most important thing is to act as if you really know a lot about it, and make sure to throw in meaningless acronyms like TTFN and SBD.

What books can I read to help me learn about the Internet?

My favorites are:

• Internet Etiquette by Emily Post

- The Joy of Internet by Alex Comfort, M.D.
- Kermit and the Internet by Miss Piggy.com

How did you become such an expert on this topic?

I learned from my children. All kids, including mine, now are born with the techno-gene. This explains why they can understand the most sophisticated electronic systems even when they can't figure out how to take off their clothes without turning them inside out.

Will I one day be able to access the Internet through my TV?

Yes, although in the beginning you'll only be able to get zeroes and ones. The good news is that it will still be better than most stuff on TV. You might need to use a coat hanger if the reception is poor.

How good is the security on the Internet?

It's as secure as when you told your best friend in junior high school that, "I'm going to tell you the biggest secret in the world, but you have to promise not to tell anyone!"

Now that you have enough knowledge to discuss the Internet with all plants and most animals, you can really start to use it on the job. If you have other questions that haven't been answered in this article, feel free to e-mail me at on-the-beach@waves.are.com.

HONEY, I'M HOME (BUT I'M WORKING)

December 1996/January 1997

There are some good things about working from home. One of my favorites is that I have a window office. Unfortunately, it is a window that requires cleaning, with a screen I have to repair, and it looks out on the grass that needs to be mowed. It makes it easy to plan your weekend.

TIMOTHY J. JONES

Not many people know it, but Ozzie Nelson was a trendsetter. Everyone thought he didn't work, but he was one of the first telecommuters. He had to be working at home, because he lived in a nice house, you never saw him go to work, and no one ever mentioned good old rich Uncle Wilbur (may he rest in peace). He probably had the equivalent of a laptop (which at that time would have taken up his whole rumpus room), and used it to communicate with his office.

Now many HRMS people, including me, are following in Ozzie's footsteps and telecommuting at least part of the time. Just like basketball players all appearing to be over eight-feet tall, it's a trend that seems to be growing.

When some people think of telecommuting, they think of being able to walk into their home office without commuting headaches, working in comfortable clothes, and being highly productive because they can work without people plopping down unannounced in their office. This is all true, but telecommuters must expect hardships such as these if they want to make a living in a tough world.

As anyone who has telecommuted knows, it's different from being in a "regular" office. One time, for instance, I had to put a call on hold when my son Tommy, who was then three and already potty trained but not quite self-sufficient, called out from the bathroom "I'm done!!!" Unless the phone call involves a deal at least as big as selling the entire state of Montana, you cannot leave a three-year-old to fend for themselves in that situation. If you do, your office might be paperless, but the rest of the house would not.

Along with adjusting to different working conditions, telecommuters need to sharpen their interpersonal skills. Since telecommuters deal with people mainly on the phone and through e-mail, rather than face-to-face, they need to develop a high level of empathy for the people they're working with. For example, a telecommuter calls someone at a downtown office early in the morning:

Telecommuter (sitting in an old sweatsuit, with coffee and a warm muffin): "So how's your morning going so far?"

Real commuter (after an hour in bumper-to-bumper traffic): "Y-a-a-a-a-i-i-i-e-e-e!!!!!!!!!!!!"

Telecommuter (showing empathy): "That's good. I love working at home."

Since telecommuters never meet a lot of the people they work with, no one knows what they look like. When people ask, I tell them I resemble Robert Redford, even though it's more like Woody Allen.

Another adjustment that telecommuters have to make is on

Take Your Daughter to Work Day, because they have to take their daughters to where someone else works. I believe it's an important day, so next year, I think I'll take my daughter to where the Chicago Cubs work and spend the day at Wrigley Field.

You also have to change some long-time habits when you telecommute. You can't, for instance, complain about the company cafeteria. You also have to realize that your waste paper basket doesn't empty itself.

Although kids can sometimes rise to the top of a telecommuter's to-do list, you can use the situation to your advantage in the ongoing battle to keep their noise level somewhat below that of an airport runway. "Keep it down," my wife will say. "Daddy's working."

"But he's in the *shower*." (It doesn't work all the time.)

A big advantage of telecommuting is that your home workspace gives you a place to display whatever stuff you want. Most people, no matter how discriminating, have some personal item or piece of art that is so ugly that it looks like a half-eaten room service meal left out in the hallway overnight. If you telecommute, you can put it, along with all the unidentified pottery-like objects your kids have made, in your home office.

Telecommuting involves a fundamental change in the way people work. As HRMS professionals whose skills will be needed to effect this monumental transformation, we have an obligation to ensure that we provide telecommuters with the tools and knowledge to be successful. I recommend we start with Rule #1: *"Don't make a phone call if you see a three-year-old go into the bathroom."*

It's Here! It's Cool! It's...HRMS-TV!

February/March 1997

Remember when you were a kid and your parents would tell you to turn off the TV? With some of the stuff that's on now, no one has to tell me that. But a new network promises to rekindle that old excitement.

I've just received my greatest honor as a member of the well-respected profession of Media Person. I say "well respected" because of our contributions to humanity such as the National Enquirer and reality TV.

The honor is that I was asked to preview the shows on a new cable channel, HRMS-TV. At first I was surprised there would be such a channel, but when I realized there are channels devoted to things such as gardening, cartoons, and zucchini (Zuke TV), I thought: "Why not us?"

I always wondered how critics manage to keep from blurting out the ending of the exciting shows they've watched. Can you imagine if you knew, in advance, who shot J.R., and you weren't allowed to tell? That would be almost impossible, and dangerous. If I'd known the secret, I would have had Secret Service protection in case a crazed couch potato threatened to mash me if I didn't tell.

Anyway, here's the scoop on the new shows that will soon be coming right at you (don't forget to duck):

"Techno Tool Town" shows the fun we can have with the week's featured piece of hardware or software. On this show, the host uses the techno tool of the week to do something interesting, such as downloading top-secret national security documents and putting them on the Internet.

A gritty, seamier-side-of-life show is "CyberJail." In this show, HR data is locked in a seemingly secure prison, and hackers try to help it escape. The viewer is kept in suspense until the end, when this sophisticated password generator, disguised as a benefit plan code, slips into the jail and... Oops, I almost gave it away, but my lips are sealed. You'll have to beat it out of me with a hard drive.

There's a game show called "Wheel of Buzzwords." On this fast-paced show, contestants try to guess the latest technical terms by exposing one letter at a time. The show is interesting until the end, when the answer is revealed and the audience yells "that's already obsolete."

One of the more suspenseful shows is "Mission You Gotta Be Kidding," where members of the Information Management (IM) force try to solve HR system problems that threaten the world. It's very cleverly done, with the characters using such spy-type tools as masks (numbers disguised as "Zs"), secret codes (like "B" for biweekly), and explosives (programs blowing up). The special agents are sometimes joined by The Woman from A.U.N.T. (Association of Unix and NT).

There is a variety show that takes you back to the wild and wacky 1970s, hosted by Sonny and Cher impersonators. The show has great acts, such as the Data Pointer Sisters, the conversion-tool group Boyz II Men, and the detective who started the Internet, Jack "Worldwide" Webb. In keeping with the network's computer theme, Cher is dressed as a "1," and Sonny is a zero.

As you can imagine, HRMS-TV won't have any problem finding sponsors. Knowing that our organization will want to be included, I've already written a jingle:

We're the group that's just for you,
HR, systems, payroll too.
Did you ever try to rhy-em
With a word that sounds like IHRIM?

I also thought our journal would want to advertise, and it can use this little ditty:

What's the publication that is made for you and me?
I-H-R-I-M-l-i-n-k dee dee.

As you can tell, this new network is a can't-miss thing. If you sign up in the next 30 days, they'll send you a poster of Sonny and Cher, and as an added incentive, if you're one of the first 100 subscribers, you don't have to take the poster. Call your cable company today and tell them you want your HRMS-TV, and you want it now.

HEY, YOU'RE GOOD!

April/May 1997

Whenever you have self-doubts, there's one thing that should always make you realize how terrific you are — your résumé. The person described there is a star, and it must be you, because it has your name on it. Hopefully, it's someone you recognize.

For many reasons, it seems that people change jobs today almost as often as they change their socks. I even know someone who changes jobs *more* often than his socks, but since he's been at the same job for 10 years, I've kept in touch only by e-mail.

The same is true for us in HRMS (the "jobs" part, not the "socks" part, I hope), but we face the additional challenge of all people in the technology field. Put simply, many jobs require five years of experience with technology that is only one month old.

This situation has made it more difficult to create a good résumé, but never fear. With the tips provided in this article, you will be able to compose one that will land you your dream job, which for me would be senior grass growing watcher at Fenway Park during baseball season.

You may wonder how I know so much about résumés. I acquired my extensive knowledge in my recent experience advising Katie, my eight-year-old, on how to create one. We did this because she asked me to buy her the Dennis Rodman Barbie/Ken doll, and I suggested she get a job and buy it herself.

Katie liked that idea, so we started working on her résumé. We began by considering what she was good at. We came up with: getting Tommy (her five-year-old brother) to do stuff for her, playing with new toys but only for a short time, and leaving one mess to start on another. Needless to say, it wasn't long before she

obtained a management position.

Now as you consider your own résumé, remember that its only purpose is to make you sound so wonderful that someone wants to see you. And who are the best people in the world at doing this? That's right — realtors.

If you have recently been looking for a house, you may have realized that many of those you looked at were houses you would never have looked at if it hadn't been for the glowing description. But the important point is that the words convinced you to take a look.

As a training example, let's use "realtor-talk" to describe a deserted old farmhouse that's missing the doors and windows:

"Lots of history in this beauty. Perfect for those who love the feel of the outdoors. Plenty of cross-breezes."

See, it's simple. Now let's apply this thinking to résumés, and as we do we'll adapt it to HRMS. What this means is that, other than your name, the rest of your résumé should be acronyms and buzzwords. In fact, if it takes less than 10 minutes to get it through your spell checker, you are not finished.

To illustrate how easy it is to compose an irresistible résumé, let's examine your skills. Are you good at serious quiet listening? Then you are strong in SQL. Have you ever made small talk at a party? OK, you're an expert in Smalltalk (so big deal, you committed a "capital" offense). Do you wear BVDs? Put it on your résumé, and if anyone asks what it is, just say it's software.

These are excellent points, you are now thinking, but they also present the slight problem that you will be saying you are good at something that you know nothing about. And this may concern you.

Don't worry. With technology changing so fast, there is a good chance that whatever you said you were good at will no longer be in use at the company by the time you start your new job. Your first assignment will probably be to learn something that is so new that you couldn't possibly have had that knowledge when you got the job offer.

So instead of worrying if you have today's skills, take comfort in the fact that the really desirable skills are tomorrow's, and *no one* has them. But if you're still worried, you can always use Katie's résumé, but don't write it with crayons.

WE'VE COME A LONG WAY

June/July 1997

Over the years, HR systems people have built a profession where none existed. It's good every once in a while to take a minute and appreciate what we have accomplished... OK, your minute's up — get back to work.

It's hard to know how far we've progressed with HR systems until we consider how things used to be. I use this approach with my kids when I tell them how we had to walk eight miles in the snow to school, uphill in both directions. They look at me in admiration and say something like, "Gee Dad, that's *stupid*." I pat myself on the back for taking advantage of that teachable moment.

It may be hard for some people in HRMS to realize that there was once a time when there wasn't any "HR," and there weren't any real "MSs." Those were the days before PCs, when personnel information was kept in "FCs" (filing cabinets). I'm not longing for those days, of course, but it made you feel secure to look at those cabinets and know all the useful information that was in them.

When I say "useful," however, I'm not thinking of the literal meaning such as actually able to be used. With all that paper, we still couldn't answer critical questions such as "how many people in our department played basketball in college," and then use the information for the business purpose of forming an unbeatable team for the company picnic.

And it was because of this shortfall, where our teams lost so many times, that we developed HR systems and started doing ad hoc reports. Now these weren't just any reports. These were special reports, and you could tell because it took a week to produce them. And when they were done, the recipient would be grateful and say something like "can you sort this another way?," which would take only another couple of days. But I can tell I'm getting too nostalgic.

As unbelievable as it might sound to some people, there was a time when HR "users" would do absolutely *anything* to make nice-nice to a programmer just to see employee information. As a well-dressed programmer in those days, I was a sucker for users complimenting me on my plaid pants, which I am saving for the time when they are again in style.

Those were also the days when users and programmers rarely talked to each other, the main reason being that most of their conversations went something like this:

User: "Hi."
Programmer: "What do you want from me?"
User: "Nothing, I'm just saying hi."
Programmer (warily): "Okay, hi."
User: "Great game yesterday."
Programmer: "We got a new mainframe last week."
User: "I didn't think we'd pull it out until that last touchdown."
Programmer: "Now we can run payroll in less than two days."

User: "Now that I have you, there's just one thing I'd like to ask if it would be a big deal to do."

Programmer: "I thought so. What do you want?"

User: "I can't describe it, but I'll know it when I see it."

Some people may think this conversation couldn't have happened, but I found it in a little-read book called *Users are From Mars, Programmers are From Venus.*

But that's all in the distant past, and we now live in different times. It's fun to look back, but it wasn't easy working in a time of scarce technical resources, when business problems took too long to solve and even our best computers weren't quite fast enough.

Oh, well, enough about work. I'm going out tonight, so I'll go get my Nehru jacket out of the closet.

It's Everywhere, It's Everywhere!

August/September 1997

Data today isn't confined to the millions of computers in which it resides. A lot of it has left those locations to embark on wireless journeys and is literally all around us. It's only a matter of time before some piece of data realizes they've got us outnumbered, and like one of those old police TV shows, stands outside our office and yells through a megaphone, "You are surrounded. Come out with your hands up."

Remember when you were 14 years old and you thought that everyone knew more than you did about something that was really important to you? And don't you still feel that way sometimes, except it's about having the information you need to manage the HR systems function?

I don't think that feeling today comes so much from ignorance as from being overwhelmed. It used to be that the amount of available information was manageable, but now there's so much it can't even fit in William Buckley's head.

How could this have happened in such a short time? If you missed the last issue of *Computers and Canines: The Magazine for Bytes and Barks*, you might not have seen the latest research in this area. In a discovery that was startling, but that now seems perfectly logical, the noted Scientist Formerly Known As Prince determined that there is a data gene that is composed of a "0" and a "1" chromosome. (He also discovered that it's the "0" chromosome that determines if the data will ever stop to ask for directions, or if it will instead drive around in circles for hours saying "I know exactly where we are.") In scientific terms, these data chromosomes can be described as teensy weensy, but they are prolific. They reproduce by way of unsuspecting people, obtaining their pleasure vicariously while marching forward on their mission of world domination.

Of course, we should have suspected something like this in the days when the major method of creating more data was through copiers and the corporate departments that did this job were called reproduction services. But we were innocent then, and we weren't assaulted daily by the media with graphic examples of raw data.

Not only were we innocent, but the data population was under control. Whatever we needed was contained in desks and cabinets and a few computers. And then the permissive times came and *wham*, it was everywhere! It's as if these "0's" and "1's" were just waiting for the chance to do it, and now there's no stopping them.

How did it all start? There are many theories about this. One is that at first there was just a "0," and then somehow a "1" came out of it. Another is that it started out as a bunch of individual dots that over time evolved into "0's" and "1's." A third is that there was a big disk crash and all the data that will ever exist was thrown out into the universe, just waiting to be discovered.

No matter how it was originally created, data used to increase at a manageable rate, usually one file at a time. Then the fertility tool of e-mail came along. Multiple data births became much more common, as the same information could easily be sent to thousands of other locations, where it could be stored forever.

It's become obvious that if we don't do something to control the rate of data conception, we will soon have lots of little data running around with not enough space. Those "0's" and "1's" have conditioned us to enjoy creating them, with the result that we have become a bunch of data-makers, reproducing it at an alarming rate.

The only answer is self-control. Next time you get in the mood to make a little data, ask yourself, "Could I live without it just this once? And if I decide to go ahead with it, am I willing to take responsibility for it, to store it and care for it as long as it needs me?"

We're all in this together. As a public service, I urge you to be responsible with your data storage methods and practice safe hex.

HRMS Under the Big Top

October/November 1997

It's always fun to go to the circus. When we're watching it, with acts ranging from dangerous to unusual to funny, I suspect everyone has a similar thought — "what would it be like to work there as an HR systems person?"

Some kids want to join the circus when they grow up. I was a little different, and I don't say this just because I had a pet slide rule that I walked twice a day. When I was a kid, I always wanted to be an HR systems person. Recently I had a chance to speak with someone who is doing both.

In my search for untraditional uses of human resource systems, I interviewed the HRMS manager for a traveling circus, L. E. Fint (I know, sometimes I'm so transparent that, as Yogi Berra might say, you can see right over me). Listen in:

Future Pulitzer Prize winning journalist (that's me): Can you tell me a little about your HRMS?

L. E. Fint: We call it 3RINGS, which stands for 3-part Really INGenious System. Its major functions are the balancing of payroll, the juggling of HR, and the safety net of benefits.

FPPWJ: It must be fun to work in a circus.

LEF: It sure is, but sometimes our work is intense. Get it, in tents! Ha, ha! Isn't that a hoot?

FPPWJ: Oh, yeah, sure. What are some of the unusual aspects of a circus's HRMS?

LEF: We think of the animals as employees, so we have them in the database, along with the people.

FPPWJ: That must create some unusual situations.

LEF: It sure does. Like the way we use the salary field, because our elephants work for peanuts. (Canned laughter in the background.) Oh, I'm so funny I can hardly stand it.

FPPWJ: I'm with you there. You didn't happen to ever want to be a clown, did you?

LEF: I did, but I went into HRMS so I could wear funny clothes. Oh, I'm such a stitch!!

FPPWJ: Sew you are. What else is unusual about your HRMS?

LEF: Like most circuses, many of our people have multiple jobs, and we need to store that information. For example, one of our employees is Stretcho, the world's tallest man. He's also Fifi, one of those little poodles in our dog act.

FPPWJ: How does he do that?

LEF: We have great makeup people.

FPPWJ: Who else does more than one job?

LEF: Well, there's Pretzel Man, who can twist himself into all sorts of positions. He also administers our flexible benefits.

FPPWJ: Do you have any jobs other than HRMS manager?

LEF: Yes, I'm also the director of back end processing.

FPPWJ: That sounds technical. What is it?

LEF: I follow behind the horses, and when they go...

FPPWJ: Thanks. I get the picture. How did you end up with that job?

LEF: One day we had a problem with our HRMS, and when I said "garbage in, garbage out," our ringmaster said, "I have the perfect job for you."

FPPWJ: It sounds like a good match. Hey, thanks for your time.

LEF: Sure thing. I've gotta go anyway. It's time to walk Stretcho.

CENTURY DATE—
THE EVERY-100-YEAR WAR

December 1997/January 1998

Now that we know the year 2000 came and went with relatively few system problems, it's hard to remember how big an issue it was in the late 1990s. When I look back, I remember it mainly for the great benefit it provided — full employment for COBOL programmers.

What is this, another article about *the Y2K problem*? Those were my thoughts too when I read one a few months ago in my hometown newspaper, the *Champaign-Urbana News-Gazette* (once voted the best newspaper in the entire sprawling metropolis of Champaign-Urbana). The reporter wrote it (and I am not making this up) as if he had *just uncovered* the issue and was rushing to tell an unsuspecting public so we could immediately take protective action. The article had the same tone as if the writer had just discovered plans for an imminent alien invasion. Its hard-hitting conclusion was that this issue is more than merely adding a couple of digits to date fields, and it's a really big problem that has never occurred before.

Everyone in HRMS knows this is a very big issue, but that insightful article (as measured on the *d-u-h!* meter that my children apply to everything I say) scared me into wanting to know more. Since I live near the University of Illinois and often do extensive research for this column (including once renting the Addams Family movie and watching the *whole thing*), I frequently take advantage of the wonderful university facilities. The fact that these facilities normally consist of the basketball arena, student union food court, and the bowling alley does not lessen my feeling of being scholarly.

But this time, I actually went to the library, and following my normal highly-focused research routine, I spent about two hours reading the first baseball book I found and called it a day. On my next trip, however, I found an article from 1899 in the business section. It discussed how difficult it would be to change to the year 1900 in the new industrialized society. The author concluded that it was much more complicated than just changing the dates on all the paper forms being used, and that this was a monumental problem that we've never had to solve. The article even mentioned legislation introduced by U.S. Senator Strom Thurmond (R-S.C.) to help solve it, one of the lesser-known bills in his long-lasting Senate career.

This gave me a different perspective on the issue, so I kept looking. In the communications section, I found a flyer from the year 1499. It said that there had been many items printed since the invention of the printing press, and that the year 1500 would create a major need to redo a lot of them. The flyer said that this involved more than just a few pieces of paper, and that it was a huge problem. It also stated that it was unique in the history of the world, but that maybe the minister of licenses for explorers, Strom Thurmond (R-New World), could help.

Now I was even more curious, so I continued digging back in the really old stuff. And you won't believe what I found (mostly because I'm using my favorite journalistic technique called "making it up"). For the year 199 A.D., I found the session descriptions from the annual conference of The Roman Empire Guild of People-Counting Professionals, the forerunner of HRSP and IHRIM. One of the sessions was titled "The Year 200 Issue," and it was led by the vice-emperor of stones and cubits, Strom Thurmond (R-Babylon). The description said that the issue involved more than just adding another bead to the abacus, and that "it is a problemus largeus that has never happened a priorius."

I guess every 100 years we have to solve some of the same problems we did the last time, plus a lot more. I don't know about you, but I've learned my lesson from this century date thing, and I won't make the same mistakes next time. And just to be sure, when we get close to it, I'll consult with Strom III (R-Neptune).

And What Do You Do? Oh, How Interesting

February/March 1998

Did you ever wish you had a job that was easy to explain? I had one once, but it got boring, so I decided to quit playing center field for the Yankees and enter the world of HRMS.

Every day, those of us in HRMS deal with significant issues such as adapting to rapidly changing technology, doing more with less, and complying with increasing regulatory requirements. But these are easy compared to our most critical issue, which is "How do we describe our jobs to people we meet at parties?"

Of course, it isn't only at social functions where people have no idea what we do. To my neighbors, all of whom have jobs like teacher, doctor and small business owner, I have the "mystery job." They probably suspect there's a cone of silence in my house and that my wife is really "99." (Would you believe 98? How about 6 3/4?)

At family gatherings, I have had many pleasant conversations about my work over the last 20 years. Unfortunately, the only thing I've said that has made sense is that "I work with computers." Even though this is true of just about everyone, from auto mechanics to nuclear physicists, that statement lets us both understand exactly what I do. It's just a different understanding.

Fortunately, I have no such problem with my wife, whose field is the systems area of judicial administration. Her profession is a lot like ours, except with criminals instead of employees. But where we get to deal with exciting topics such as imputed income, she has to settle for boring courtroom action such as viewing films confiscated as evidence in obscenity trials.

But most people are not like my wife, and our profession is difficult for them to understand. At least I can talk about crabgrass with neighbors, and my family is always interested in the children, but it's at parties, where a person's occupation is a normal ice-breaker, where the problem is the worst. How many times have you had a conversation like this?:

Me: Hi, my name is Elliott (*you would substitute your own name*).
Person with an easy-to-explain job: Nice to meet you. I'm Bob.
Me: And what do you do?
Bob: I clean out septic tanks.
Me: That's very interesting. (*I now know exactly what Bob does. I don't want to talk about it, but at least I know. And Bob is so sure of himself because he has a job that everyone understands. It gives him a certain aura, but now I notice there is more to that aura than you might think.*)
Bob: And what do you do?
Me: I work in human resource systems.
Bob: Oh. (*I've heard this "Oh" before, and I know it means he has no idea what I do, but since he's polite, he will at least try.*) That sounds interesting. What's that?
Me (*taking my one shot at it and trying to make it simple*): I work with computer systems that gather, store, process, disseminate and analyze information relating to employees, retirees,

applicants and other organizational constituencies, regarding their employment-related activities in areas such as human resources, benefits and payroll. (*I'm fortunate to have the gift of making things understandable. Not everyone is so lucky.*)

Bob: That's nice. It sounds like our work is a lot alike. By the way, when was the last time you took a close look at your septic tank?

I'm sure this situation is all too familiar, and you're wondering how you can avoid it next time. Well, I have solved this problem. Now when I meet someone at a party and they ask what I do, I put on my serious face, look all around to make sure no one else can hear, and in a voice barely above a whisper I tell them, "I'm Elvis, but don't tell anyone." They still say "Oh," but it's a very different "Oh," and it must be working, because no one has ever asked me to explain. I guess it gives me a certain aura.

On the Serious Side

April/May 1998

There's some great stuff to read out there: War and Peace, A Tale of Two Cities, Crime and Punishment...*I could go on and on about things I haven't read. But I do enjoy reading, as long as the author doesn't get all show-offy and use big words like karyotype (the chromosomal complement of an individual or of a species). I can't stand when they do that.*

Now that I've written "The Back Page" for four years, my wife suggested it was time I write something more businesslike, or else she thinks no one will take me seriously. I know this is true, at least based on how effective I am in communicating with my kids. They give me that "eye-roll" whenever I say something wise to them, such as "be careful or your face will freeze like that."

To counter this image, I tried to think of a valuable service I could provide to people in the HRMS field. At the same time, I hope I don't disappoint regular readers of this column who are expecting another side-splitting piece. But don't worry, the supposedly funny stuff will be back next time, ghost-written by Dave Barry as usual. (He sends me all his good work and uses the leftovers for his column.)

Knowing that everyone wants to maximize the productivity of their professional reading time, I thought I'd list some of the journals and newspapers I use to keep up with what's going on in our business and with business in general. I invite all of you to let me know of others.

One of my favorite technology journals is *Byte-Size*. It's for short people in the HRMS field, which is perfect for me. A nice thing is that it's always stocked on the bottom shelf.

To keep up with what's going on in human resources, I read H "R" Us. In addition to the insightful articles, my kids like the pictures.

For the latest on business, I read a Memphis financial newspaper called *The Tennessee Waltz Street Journal*. I especially like the articles by their beat writer, and my favorite column is called "Balance Sheet Music."

To make the best use of my time, I like the *Reader's Digest Guide to New Technology Products*. The articles are condensed to convey only the important information. They tell you that the products work with operating systems, data base management systems, and hardware, but they don't tell you which ones, so you don't get caught up in a lot of detail.

For some really fun reading, there is an unusual publication that focuses on the latest buzzwords. Last month it was called *Cyber-Systonics*, but in keeping with its theme, the name is changed each time to something else that no one understands.

A relatively new journal I like is *PC/PC: Politically Correct Personal Computing*. You can get answers to those sticky online etiquette questions from columnists LAN Anders and Emily Post-it Notes.

Most of what I read I would show to my kids (hoping they can explain it to me), but not *Technology Uncovered*. This glossy magazine covers topics such as explicit holography and stripped-down versions of products. They really go too far, but I figure if I buy it, that's one copy I've kept out of a young person's hands.

I'm sure these publications will help you in your career. I have enjoyed making this contribution to the betterment of our planet so much that I am thinking of moving on to bigger things. For the next column, I'm considering describing how I was able to create life using only products advertised in *IHRIM.link*, along with some DNA I found under the sofa cushions.

The Free PC
(by Dr. Suess-tems Analyst)

June/July 1998

When you buy a PC, you're not just getting a computer. You are acquiring something with endless possibilities for add-ons, upgrades and accessories. It's like the adult equivalent of Barbie.

With admiration for the real Dr. Suess, who I wish had written technical manuals:

A friend that I know had an extra PC,
And since he's so nice he just gave it to me!
A CPU, monitor, keyboard for free!!
And little drive A, and little drive C.

And he gave me, to save my screen,
A woman waving, she's a queen,
Atop a bright green concrete paver.
It was quite keen, a special favor.
It's one that I will always savor,
This queen waver, green paver, keen favor screen saver.

But, before my PC starts
He said that it would need some parts.
The first one was a cyber snoot-up,
Needed so that it could boot up.

And then, the software is required.
Now here's where you can get inspired.
You can buy stuff off the shelf

Or write the code all by yourself.

Of course, you have to buy the shelf stuff,
And you have to write the self stuff.
Each will cost in its own way,
With one you work, with one you pay.

And next he said I'd want to get
Something for the Internet.
For this I'd need a zimperfam
To surf from Minsk to Rotterdam.

Now these are not too hard to find.
He said, "I'd like to lend you mine,
But what I have won't work with yours.
You have Windows, I have Doors."

And next…
One thing you'll want so you have no regrets
Is something to organize all your diskettes.
'Cause if you don't get this, and wait a long while,
You'll have something awful,
A file in a pile.

Now a file in a pile is not something you want.
It's sort of like searching for one perfect font.
You'll look and you'll look for the troublesome file.
You know that it's somewhere,
The file in a pile.

Oh… another thing you'll need
Is something to improve the speed.
Your free PC's a little slow,
So buy a four-phase super-go.

And you'll want an extra gig
'Cause the hard drive's not too big.
Plus a drive for a CD,
Which isn't on your free PC.

But still,
If you go and buy all of this stuff,
You'll soon find that you just cannot have enough.
You'll always need more things
And more,
more,
more,

more.
You might as well sleep in a bed at the store.

And don't forget a surge protector,
Certified by an inspector.
Plus a 92-pin cable.
And you'll want a PC table.

Then I'm sure you'll need a printer.
Plus, this monitor's a squinter.
Get at least a 19-incher.
Never be a penny pincher.

'Cause if you are I'm sure you'll see
That you can't use your new PC.
And when you're on your spending spree,
Remember that you got it free.

HR: Funny Side Up

H.R.I.S. – He Really Isn't Square

August/September 1998

My children view parents with great admiration and as role models to help them lead a happy, productive life. The one thing I don't understand, though, is why they feel this way only about their friends' parents.

Last spring there was a special afternoon at my children's elementary school when parents were invited to talk to the kids about their jobs. Oh good, I thought, I'll do it. My work is at least as interesting to youngsters as that of many of the other speakers I saw listed, such as hot air balloon pilot, police detective and pet shop owner.

When I told Katie, my third grader, that I wanted to talk about human resource management systems, she quickly replied "Yeah, right. What are you going to show them, Dad? My friends would *love* to watch you read your e-mail." I don't know what they're teaching them at school now, but that has to be where they get this smart-alecky stuff. I know it can't be from home.

"No, smarty-pants," I said. "I'm going to let them watch me use technology to help companies acquire a competitive advantage with their human resource systems." (Pretty clever, I'm thinking. I'll be the star of the program. Her friends will love it.)

"My friends will *hate* it!" she wailed. "I'll just *die*!"

OK, I can take a hint. But it did get me thinking. If my kids think that what I do is so uncool (or whatever word they're using now), how can we encourage these precious little angels, our future payers of Social Security to allow us to retire, to enter our field?

First, I can't accept that human resource systems is a square profession, because that would make me, uh, you know, old. (I know it's not true, because I still listen to my Jimi Hendrix albums, even if they're scratchy.) But I can accept that maybe we could make it seem groovier to kids. And I think I'm just the guy who can do it. You may not know this, but they call me "the sporty guy." By "they," I mean my friends in the Let's Go Watch the Corn Grow Club.

So I thought about next year's event at the kids' school, and I'll be ready. I'll start my session by asking, "If Britney Spears needed a human resource management system, who do you think she'd turn to?" After that opening I'd have them in the palm of my hand, and then I'd tell them they would get a chance to work with products that are Generation Next®©™(TGIF). But I think the biggest attention-grabber would be to give the talk as the famous rapper e.wit@:

I work in HR
It's the coolest by far.
You can be a star
Let me tell you who we are.

We work with data.
The job is great-a.

We print up all the paychecks,
Don't need no calculate-a.

'Cause computers work it out.
That's what we're about.
You can just relax
While the system does the tax.

So think about your future.
You'd love it in HR.
And like your favorite rapper here
You'd be a superstar.

And if Katie's friends don't want to become human resource systems professionals after that, then I'm just going to lock myself in a room, put on headphones, and crank up the volume on my favorite Peter, Paul and Mary album.

GET IT DONE RIGHT, CHEAPLY AND YESTERDAY

October/November 1998

Babe Ruth was the ultimate party animal during his baseball career. Although he wanted to be a manager, he never got the chance because, as Yankee general manager Ed Barrow said, "How can he manage a team if he can't even manage himself?" So maybe my secret motivation for wanting to be a project manager is that I can do at least one thing better than Babe Ruth.

I enjoy managing system development projects. When people ask me why, I have told them it's because it lets me do something where I can leave a reminder of myself behind when I'm done. I was pleased by this answer — so profound, so inner-revealing, so *je ne sais quoi* — until I realized that it was also how the question "why do you like going for a walk" would be answered by a dog. But then I thought even more, and I realized that answer *would* be profound for a dog, so I think I'll stick with it. But maybe I should explain a little.

I think everyone wants to do something that lets the world know "I was here." Some people can do this by building things like houses or bridges or computers. These are people who we refer to as "mechanically inclined." Those same words have often been used to describe me, such as "my parakeet is more mechanically inclined than Elliott." But I am "projectically inclined," so if I want to build something, I need to stick to managing projects.

I once heard the job described as one where everyone is allowed to make whatever requests they want, and the project manager is then expected to somehow get them all done, on time and within budget. Based on this, I think the best training for an HR/payroll systems project manager is the type that's given to people who play Santa Claus at shopping malls. I base this observation on the nature of the requests that are made of people in these two jobs, as well as the clients' expectations for delivery. The following table compares the two roles:

	Shopping mall Santa	HR/payroll systems project manager
Requestors	Cute, cuddly kids	Cute, cuddly end users, auditors, and senior management
Normal delivery date	Just before year end	Just before year end
Requestors' concerns for your staffing and budget problems	None – they figure you can always squeeze a little more out of the elves	None (see note about elves)
Visibility when things go wrong	Highly visible – just like missing a payday	Highly visible – just like missing Christmas

Along with the Santa-like aspects of the job, another part of project management that I really enjoy is status reporting. It has all the characteristics of the things I like doing — you get better at it with experience, it's more fun to do with someone else than alone, and as soon as you're finished someone wants you to do it again.

In looking for advice on how to be a good project manager, I turned to a book that I think contains a lot of useful information on a number of topics. And right *in the beginning*, there's a description of what I consider a very successful project — the creation of the world. I think it's a good project to use as a model for a number of reasons: there are lots of users, the end product has stood the test of time, and it has proven to be extremely scalable. I learned the following project management lessons, most of which are transferable to other projects:

1. *You must have a defined scope (for example, create the heavens, earth, plants, animals and people).*
2. *Allow for contingencies (even if you think it will take six days, allow an extra day just in case).*
3. *Encourage creativity.*
4. *Have all the users report directly to the project manager.*
5. This one I haven't figured out how to do yet — *Don't create the users until the project is almost over.*

Having managed many projects, I have had to fight the inclination to do too much planning in my personal life. I do have a list of every activity I expect to do between now and the year 2010, along with task durations, dependencies, and the names of all involved parties, but I don't think that's extreme. And just to make sure I don't go overboard, I have scheduled April 1, 2007 as my own spontaneity day. Maybe I'll do something wacky that day — like make up a list of tasks and then do them all, *but out of order.*

I guess that's what I really like about being a project manager. It gives me a chance to be a wild and crazy guy, as long as it's in the plan.

A Trip on the H.R.M.S. Minnow

December 1998/January 1999

Wireless technology is becoming more prevalent, and it can be extremely helpful, even critical, in some situations. At some point in the near future we will probably wonder how we ever lived without it, just as we have now come to regard the Thigh Master. But if this technology had existed in the 1960s, it would have made the plight of seven stranded castaways so implausible as to render it almost silly.

Just sit right back and you'll hear a tale,
A tale of a fateful trip.
That started from this tropic port
Aboard this tiny ship…

I hope you will be as thrilled as I was when I heard about the discovery of a lost episode of the TV show Gilligan's Island. And what made it even better was when I found out how relevant this particular one is to our profession. Here's the script from this intellectually stimulating show:

Mary Ann *(smiling her sunny Kansas farm girl smile)*: Golly gee, sometimes I just can't help wishing we could get off this island.

Gilligan: Me, too. If we don't, I'll never get to pursue my dream of working in human resource systems.

Skipper: I never knew you wanted to do that.

Gilligan: Oh yeah, Skipper. Ever since I heard they get to program in Sea.

Professor: Hey, that gives me an idea. If we developed a Web site, someone would find us and we'd be rescued.

Mary Ann: I know I'm just a Kansas farm girl, but it doesn't make sense to me how we could do that.

Professor: Logically you're correct, but this whole show never

made sense, and people still loved to watch it.

Ginger: I need to change into another of the many outfits I brought with me on a three-hour tour, a three-hour tour. *(She walks to her hut.)*

Professor: See what I mean about the show not making any sense. How did Ginger get all those clothes? OK, let's get to work on that Web site.

Mr. Howell: Why don't we just buy one? I'll take mine with caviar.

Mrs. Howell: Oh, Thurston, you're so smart.

Ginger returns wearing a ballroom gown from the 1700s.

Professor: First, we'll need a computer. If we use some special bananas that grow in just one place on the island, and attach them to this magnet I just happen to have, and run it with solar energy, we can build a Pentium 2.2 gigahertz with an 80 gig hard drive and 512K of RAM.

Mary Ann: That's another thing that never made any sense, that the Professor could build anything we needed. And he knew *everything* about *everything*.

Gilligan: I'll go get those special bananas that grow in just one place on the island.

Ginger: I'll be right back after I change. *(She walks to her hut.)*

Skipper: How will you key in the code for the Web site?

Professor: That's simple, Skipper. I'll make some drums, beat on them in hexadecimal, and convert the sound waves to Visual Basic. All I need is the bark from a palm tree and some sodium trichlorethylide, which fortunately is abundant on this island but isn't found anywhere else in the world.

Mrs. Howell: Oh, Thurston, this is so exciting. We're going to be rescued.

Mr. Howell: And just in time for the polo season, Lovey. This year, let's buy all the horses so ours is sure to win.

Skipper: I wonder what's keeping my little buddy with those special bananas. After all, you can't go very far on a small, fake island.

Gilligan comes out of the woods, carrying bananas. Just before he gets to the Professor, he trips and smashes them all.

Skipper: Oh, Gilligan, look what you've done. Now we'll never be able to develop that Web site and get off the island.

Gilligan: I'm sorry, Skipper. (Sheepish grin.) Does anyone want a banana split?

So join us here each week my friends,
You're sure to get a smile,
From seven stranded castaways,
Here on Gilligan's I-i-i-sle.

THE WRITE STUFF

February/March 1999

Most of us who write do so simply for the fun of it. Very few people can write a best-seller unless they have exceptional ability, such as the ability to be a presidential intern and then write about their experiences. I realized long ago that I couldn't compete with that level of talent.

I recently received an e-mail which read:

I love your writing. I think you are the most talented writer in the world. How can I learn to write even half as well as you?

I was very glad to get this note, because it showed me that, if you send e-mail to yourself, it's almost instantaneous.

But as with the many other notes I get, such as the pleading ones from editors ("Please do not send me any more of your stuff"), it got me thinking about how I could help others break into the multi-million dollar world of writing about HR systems.

If this is your dream, there are some steps you can take so that you are at least as successful as someone trying to sell ice in Alaska. Your first step is to become an expert in one or more aspects of the field. For my specialties, I have chosen mainframe systems, PC-based systems, Web-enabled systems, compensation, benefits, organizational development, employment, payroll processing, taxation, long-range planning, short-range planning, in-the-middle planning and project management. You should develop your own highly selective list.

After you have the knowledge, you must next develop your writing skills. You will need to acquire an eye for the mostest finest aspects of writing, including, but not limited to, eliminating redundancies, avoiding unnecessary words, and taking too long to express a thought that can be expressed in a shorter space, and also, you will need to avoid run-on sentences and long, rambling sentences, and also, you must learn to avoid redundancy. Enough said about that topic. At least for now. Or maybe even later.

I think the best way to improve your writing is to read good writing. My favorite is what I find on snack food bags, but if you are more interested in the classics, I can provide you with an attractively bound edition of *The Great Writings of Elliott Witkin*. For only US$999.99, you can have this treasure, plus one additional WriterzAid™ of your choice from the following list:

- A pad of paper from one of a wide selection of hotels, or
- A pencil from Vacation World (two in stock).

As you read some of this great writing, you will learn many techniques. One of my favorites is to use fancy fonts, which in addition to catching the reader's attention, also disguises the times when I have nothing worthwhile to say. For instance, which of these sentences do you find most interesting:

- Please pass the butter and then let's have salad.
- Please pass the butter and then let's have **sex**.

Notice how the change in font grabs your attention.

Finally, after you become a good writer you will need to learn how to market your work, because as Hamlet says in the second act of *Romeo and Juliet*, "If you're the only one who readeth your writing, you might as well have spenteth your time watching reruns of Let's Make a Deal." And if you want to learn how to find a publisher for your writing, you need to know how to avoid people who prey on ~~unsuspecting writers with no talent~~ talented writers looking for their big break. I highly recommend *Elliott Witkin Publishing University (EW-PU)*. It's a correspondence course, and although the writing is a little hard to follow, it's a terrific bargain even at half the price. It has certainly done wonders for my writing career, and for just US$999.99, it can do the same for yours. As an added bonus, the receipt for payment will say whatever is necessary so that it can be approved on your expense report, allowing it to also serve as Lesson 1 in the section on creative writing.

Once you have devoted yourself to acquiring expert knowledge, honing your writing skills and becoming a marketing whiz, you will be on your way. It will take a lot of effort, but it's worth it. I don't mean to brag, but I expect to be able to retire on my royalties (along with savings, Social Security and pensions, and maybe a part-time job) by the time I'm 80. So get going today, and *spare no expense* in striving for your goal.

BUILD A BETTER MOUSE, AND THEY WILL BUY IT

April/May 1999

The variety of software packages available is extraordinary. They range from the "what a great idea" (find directions to anywhere in the world) to the "wow, that's strange" (this was copied from an actual Web site: "This is a small software that shall drive the mosquitoes away fast. Simple to use and useful. No need for any external devices.") So if you want to develop and sell your software, I say "go for it." You can't possibly develop anything weirder than what is already out there.

If I was rich, I'd spend a lot of time writing. I would hire a staff, and their job would be to read my stuff and then laugh and tell me how funny it is. The first people I'd employ would be the editors who have sent me notes that say, "Your stuff is so bad it makes me laugh." There are definitely some good things about having money.

Unfortunately, just dreaming about being rich doesn't get you there, but I have a sure-fire plan that is based on two facts. The first is that millions of people own PCs. And the second is that PCs run software, some of which people actually buy. Based on these facts, I did some complex calculations, and they revealed that any number of dollars times any number of millions is a really big number, bigger even than some professional athletes make in a month.

Armed with this knowledge, all that was left was the small step of developing a software package that everyone wants to buy. So I worked up some ideas, and I will share them with you, but only if you promise not to tell anyone. Before you read any further, please sign the statement below and return it to me.

I acknowledge that this is a great and clever article, but I will not use it for any purpose outside of the bathroom.

Pay to the order of Elliott Witkin US$10,000

_____

Signature

You may now continue.

Here are some ideas I have for software packages:

- DOS Floss – To use this package, you would enter the dates of your previous and next dental appointments. Then it would produce a report listing all the times you should have flossed, but the heading would be (and here's where the product is so valuable) "All The Times I Really Did Floss, No Fooling, Really I Did." You can bring the report to your next appointment as evidence.

- @closet.org.anizer – This package would create a graphic representation of your closet, and let you indicate what you have thrown in there. It would contain icons representing things like clothes that are your "other" size (a size you *could* be in a month if you really wanted), ties that might one day be back in style, and gifts your kids gave you when they were in pre-school.

- Total Ctrl-Alt-Del – Any time you make a mistake at anything in your life (like forgetting your wedding anniversary or missing a deadline at work), you could use this package to let you start over.

Now that you see there are lots of possibilities, I will give you some additional tips. Specifically, these are ideas of what *not* to do, and I base these on real-life examples:

- Do not build in features such as if someone wants to tab backwards, they have to know to press **Shift Ctrl Home Tab Z.**
- When someone starts up the package, do not display (and I have actually seen something like this) "Only use this product if you trust *name of vendor* to make the assertion that this product works correctly." (I left out the vendor's name, as I don't want to incur a big **BILL** if I open the flood **GATES** for any litigation. I suspect this company's attorneys might be somewhat superior to my personal mouthpiece, who had to stretch his legal talent just to handle the sale of my house.)

OK, I've shared my ideas with you, but they're our little secret. And just in case you forget that part, you should know that I'm working on my Santa Surprise package — it sees you when you're sleeping, it knows when you're awake, it knows if you've been bad or good, and it will send all the dirt on you out over the Internet.

A "U" for You

June/July 1999

Thomas Jefferson wrote the Declaration of Independence and founded the University of Virginia. His writing contains some of the most important and beautifully-crafted text ever composed:

"We hold these truths to be self-evident, that all men are created equal, that they are endowed by their Creator with certain unalienable rights, that among these are life, liberty and the pursuit of happiness."

Few people today can match Jefferson's written eloquence. But founding a university, now that's a different story. If the ads in matchbooks are to be believed, it seems like anyone can do that.

Recently I was walking on the campus of the University of Illinois when I came upon the location where one of its founders was buried in 1898. At the site there is a marker that contains the following inscription: "If you seek his monument, look about you." I was very touched, and it made me wonder how I, Elliott Witkin, could make a difference in the world, specifically in terms of saving money on my "final" expenses like this guy did.

As I "looked about me," the answer became obvious — start a university, and have it specialize in HRMS. In keeping with the source of my inspiration, I will call it Nillinois University, so that people can proudly say, "I am a Nillinois graduate."

At this fine institution, the curriculum will consist of core courses (HR, payroll and IT), and electives. Here's the syllabus so far:

Core Courses

HR – These courses will prepare the student to perform the essential functions of human resources management. The main teaching activity will be for professors to say, "OK, guess what I will ask for tomorrow." Once students can do this, they will have mastered the critical HR aspects of the curriculum.

Payroll – Courses will help students determine if they have the temperament to work in this discipline. In the introductory course, the entire semester-length class will consist of taking care of a baby who must be fed, changed, and put to bed on an exact schedule. None of the activities can be late or missed. The students will receive no feedback when all is going well, as the only sound they will hear is the baby crying when things aren't perfect.

IT – These classes will consist of people bringing problems to the students and expecting an immediate solution. To simulate the "real world," the problems will be presented in a language unfamiliar to the students and will include foreign terms such as *imputêd incöme* (translation: fake money), *focāl point review* (eye exam) and *àrrears* (a-behinds). The problems must be solved using tools that are less than a week old, with the expectation that the students will have to use newer, but as yet non-existent tools the next week.

Electives

History – This course will cover ancient times, as far back as 1960, when primitive peoples performed basic HRMS functions using crude tools such as punch cards, U.S. mail and chisels.

Philosophy – Students will debate workplace issues such as: "Are people motivated more by money or by intrinsic factors?" Those who want an "A" are advised to choose the "money" side, while anyone who wishes to repeat the course should choose the other position.

Ethics – The purpose will be to help students determine appropriate behavior in business situations such as the following: A customer gives you a $20 bill and doesn't realize that a second bill is attached to it. The ethical question for discussion is, "Should you tell your partner about the extra $20?"

Along with this impressive academic line-up, Nillinois will also offer an active social life. There will be fraternities and sororities, which will all be named after the newest HRMS products — Beta Beta Beta.

And what university would be complete without sports? Our team, whose nickname will be the Fightin' Floppy Disks, will have the benefit of this inspiring cheer, which will immediately intimidate our opponents:

Two, four, six, eight,
We know how to calculate,
Checks,
Deductions,
Fle-e-e-e-x benefits!
AND WE'RE GONNA **MESS YOURS UP!!!**

With hijinks such as this, you would think the school would come to be known as Party U. But I won't let that happen, because I know the ultimate worth of a college is measured by academics. So just in case anyone doubts that Nillinois University is a serious institution of higher learning, just remember what the big "N" over the football stadium will stand for — it will stand for "Knowledge."

HRMS – The System With a Difference

August/September 1999

Sculptors, poets, and singers have always had one favorite subject — people. Through their artistic efforts, they have attempted to capture the diversity and beauty of humankind. In a way, that's what an HRMS does. These systems might not fit the classic definition of art, but they're at least as artistic as someone who rolls in paint and then squirms around on a canvas like a human tadpole.

According to the philosopher Barney the Dinosaur, "Everyone is special in his or her own way." (For those unfamiliar with Barney, he is a purple megalizard-like creature that preys on whiney kids with gullible, weak parents who spend lots of money on his junky merchandise. And for those of you who have heard of Barney, I have lots of his stuff that I can sell you cheap.)

In HRMS we have always believed that everyone is special, and an aspect of our systems that differentiates them from all other business applications is that we have tried to capture that uniqueness. This characteristic of our systems has struck a special chord with fellow baby boomers (those people who, according to various definitions, were born roughly between 3 B.C. and 2010). We have always wanted to think of ourselves as unique and special. We demonstrated that in our youth, as we all grew our hair long and wore ripped jeans that now would be considered too crummy to use as oil change rags. We have continued expressing our uniqueness as adults by wearing dockers and driving minivans.

But, back to HRMS. As technology has changed, it has allowed us to expand our ability to capture the uniqueness of employees. Following my usual exhaustive research methods, which involve spending hours intently watching "classic" TV shows, I found some information about how HRMS has handled this issue throughout time.

At first, it wasn't easy for people in our profession. In the Paleolithic days, everyone was named "ugh," everyone's address was "cave," and it would be 10,000 years before people had social security numbers. But most people worked from their homes then and had similar jobs, so it didn't matter that our systems couldn't differentiate among them.

Since that time, however, we have been able to use our HRMS to store unique information on employees. The chart on the next page summarizes this painstaking research:

Now that you know what happened in the past, I'm sure your next question is, "OK, Mr. Smarty Pants, how will this trend play out in the future?" As my kids say, "I know, I know, I know!"

We will soon be entering what anthropologists will call the George Jetson era. During that time, three forces will dramatically affect our HRMS:

- The desire of organizations to utilize the diverse skills of their employees,
- The ability to cost-effectively store full-stream video, and
- The fact that all years will start with a "2" (author's note — this prediction has indeed come true since this column first appeared).

Nobody has realized this, but these trends will converge (like chocolate and peanut butter to create a Reese's candy) to reshape

Era	Typical employee	Employees' unique information in an HRMS
When organized work began	Fred Flintstone	Favorite "rock" band
A long time ago	People my parents' age, but not, of course, my parents, who are still young	Number of miles they walked to school in the snow when they were children
The greatest time in the history of the world – the 1960s	John Smith	Skills, licenses, memberships, the biggest fish the employee ever caught
Current times – the era that future generations will, after much thought, eventually refer to as "the 1990s"	John Smith, Maria Lopez, Kareem Abdul-Jabbar, Lu Chen, Ravi Prakash	Pictures, fingerprints, voice patterns, body piercings

our systems and allow us to store virtually any information on an employee. For instance, instead of using a simple rating to indicate an employee's ability to speak to large groups, we will be able to store video of them performing a stand-up comic routine:

"I just flew in from Los Angeles and boy, are my arms tired! What did the snake say to his wife? Let's hiss and make up! Do you know why the kindergartner took a ladder to school? He wanted to be in a higher grade!" (*The ability to store information such as this wouldn't be good for my productivity as an HRMS professional, as I could watch this hilarious routine over and over and find new things to laugh at each time.*)

We have so far only scratched the surface in using our systems to capture the infinite diversity and uniqueness that exist in today's employees. If we work together, and raise our sights toward the achievement of lofty goals, HRMS could become the profession where we get paid for watching America's Funniest Home Videos.

HR: FUNNY SIDE UP

PLEASE WELCOME THE AMBASSADOR FROM PAYROLLIA

December 1999/January 2000

I can't think of a better explanation than this. What must have happened is that when the first corporation was created, its founder allowed the departments to buddy up with their friends. Accounting chose Finance, Marketing selected Sales, and Research hooked up with Development. When it was all over, there were three lonely souls standing by themselves — HR, Payroll, and IT. So some executive VP said, "You three, you're a team. Now go get 'em." And that's what we've done.

It was just like the United Nations. But in this case, it involved the three sovereignties of Human Resources, Payroll, and Information Technology.

They had operated under a Really Fragile Peace (RFP) for 15 years, but it was time to replace their HRMS, which was the common border they shared. Their delegates gathered to work on the requirements.

The Payroids needed only one envoy, since they were in agreement among themselves. Their main goal was to protect the interests of their close allies, the Checks. The Technikians needed dual representation, as they had split into two factions — the old guard from the province of Mainframe, and the new wave from the growing harbor area of Pea Sea. The Humanites could not use a common spokesperson, and sent emissaries from the towns of Compensation, Training, Labor Relations, Benefits and Employment. It was a joke that in a gathering of five Humanites, you would have six opinions.

First, the delegates had to agree on the shape of the conference table. The Payroids wanted a square one, with each side to represent a quarter of the year. The Humanites favored a free-form one, to signify the ever-changing nature of their discipline. They settled on one with four unequal sides.

As at the United Nations, language was an obstacle. When delegates used foreign terms such as *uncôllécted* FICA and *onë-ûp job*, interpreters translated them for the other council members.

The committee tried to identify common requirements, but they were having a difficult time. When the topic turned to reporting, the Payroids brought in samples of every one of their reports. "This is what we've always used and it has worked for us for 15 years, so this is what we need," they said.

The Humanites, on the other hand, couldn't be quite that specific. "We have no idea what our customers will ask us for," they said. "Just because we produced something yesterday doesn't mean we will ever need it again. So for reporting, we have to be able to do everything."

Therefore, Joint Resolution #2769 (Documentation of Reporting Requirements) stated "the parties agree, as witnessed by their signatures, that reporting must include a set of standard reports, and also be able to do everything, including things we haven't thought of yet."

"Perfect," said the Payroids and the Humanites. The motion passed with two ayes, zero nays, and one abstention, as the Technikians hoped that reality would eventually take over.

The delegates then turned their attention to the sticky issue of maintaining employee history. The Payroids were certain of their needs. "We need to know exactly what did happen so we can recreate it," they said.

"That won't exactly work for us," said the Humanites. "We need to know what *eventually* happened, even if it's not what *really* happened."

With that statement, a long and extremely valuable philosophical discussion occurred (the transcript of which unfortunately was not preserved for future generations), resulting in Joint Resolution #2770 (History Requirements), which stated "the parties agree, as witnessed by their signatures, that history must represent what actually happened, what eventually happened, what might have happened, what didn't happen, and what anybody thought happened." The motion passed with two ayes, zero nays, and one abstention, as it didn't even make sense to the Technikians.

But now they were rewarded for their patience, as the discussion turned to technical issues. "Our leaders want the application to be object oriented, modular and denormalized," they said.

"Whatever," replied both the Payroids and Humanites, finally agreeing on something without feeling the need for a lengthy discussion.

With the pattern set, it was then just a matter of working through the remaining issues. When the final document was produced, it was as clear as the instructions for filling out an income tax form. "We've done the hard part," the delegates said. "Now all that's left is the simple task of implementing our ideas." And with that, they returned to their respective dominions, knowing that those who followed them on the project's path would long remember (make that *very long* remember) their efforts.

HERE'S THE SOLUTION – WHAT'S THE PROBLEM?

February/March 2000

If you're ever in Miami, Florida at the right time, you will see a strange sight. Any day the temperature dips into the frigid 60s, people put on their winter clothes. And I don't just mean sweaters — I'm talking North Dakota stuff. Some people wear parkas to work. The first time I saw this while I was living there, I asked someone about it, and she told me that "we have it, so we have to use it." It may be funny with clothes, but when it happens with someone wanting to use the latest technology on your project, watch out — you might get snowballed.

It seems like every day a new system development or productivity tool hits the market. These offerings, with their interactive features and slick graphics, have a quality that is relatively new for business products — they are fun to use. Now, I'm certainly in favor of fun (I have it scheduled for the second Friday each month), but these tools are so enjoyable to work with that it seems as if the goal of some projects is just to use the latest wonder-product, rather than to solve a business problem. I call this phenomenon "sisylana," which is "analysis" backwards, because when it occurs, the answer precedes the problem.

Perhaps you have been on a project like this, where the problem can be solved with something simple like a spreadsheet, but *noooooo*!!, someone does sisylana and designs a solution using a hot new tool that is truly understood by only three people in the world, none of whom are on the project.

It may seem like I think this is a bad thing, but I know that's not always the case. For example, when personal computers first came out, they were a solution in search of a problem, and their main function seemed to be to take up a lot of space on people's desks. Now, as everyone knows, PCs have been greatly improved, to the point where they take up less room.

I can understand why people try to solve problems that may not exist, as I sometimes do it at home. Last Father's Day, when my family surprised me with the adjustable crescent wrench which I had bought and wrapped for myself, I went around the house looking for anything that needed crescenting. I used my new tool even on things that don't have bolts, such as our fish.

Maybe we're like this with new development tools because that's the way we were as children with new toys. When my son Tommy was six, we bought him a Sherlock Holmes costume, and he wouldn't leave us alone until we asked him to find some things we had "lost." At my age, that's not such a good idea, as I forgot some of the items I had misplaced.

This phenomenon of using what's available, whether it's needed or not, doesn't seem to get a lot of attention in HRMS, but I bet it would if it happened in other professions. Imagine going to see a doctor for a bad cold, and having him say, "There's this great new operation for hemorrhoids, and I want to perform it on you. The only side effect is that you become more susceptible to colds." (*Note to my editor: I know I shouldn't use a hemorrhoid joke, but I couldn't help it, as I was getting a little behind in my writing.*)

It's obvious that if sisylana occurs too often in HRMS, it would waste time and money. But being an optimist, I think there's a bright side to this. I can see a new specialty emerging in the technology field, where the main job function would be to think of new problems, which could then be solved with the newest tools.

I think this would be an excellent job, as there would be no accountability for actually solving problems, only for inventing them. These folks could form a professional association — The Society for Problem Invention in Technology (SPIT). Their motto would be: "*I like my job. Fortunately, it has its problems.*"

I know you can't SPIT into the wind, so if this is the way things are going, I might as well go with the flow. The next time I am faced with a sticky business situation, I'll be prepared with a solution. I will solve it with my crescent wrench.

We Can Be Heroes Just for One Day

April/May 2000

As an HRMS professional, do you ever feel unappreciated, misunder-stood, stuck in the middle between two sides with different objectives? If you do, there's a bright side — it's good training for when you have two teenagers. At least at work, you're right some of the time.

Call your stockbroker right now, because you are going to be rich. And if you are one of my favorite people, meaning you immediately turn to *The Back Page*, then today is your reward, because you will be in on the ground floor ahead of the other readers of this journal.

Instruct your broker to invest all your retirement savings, as well as next week's grocery money, in greeting card companies. These companies are going to make immense profits because I am beginning the campaign to create a new holiday that will cause a card-buying frenzy, sort of like Pokémon but for grown-ups.

The holiday will be in honor of HRMS folks, a group for whom recognition is long overdue. I started out with the idea of making it a whole day, but based on our schedules, I have now scaled it back to its official name — *International HRMS Hour.*

I am convinced that once people all over the world become aware of the job done by HRMS people, there will be a mad rush to join the bandwagon and thank us. In fact, I expect to be overwhelmed by a Niagara Falls of retroactive appreciation, which I am convinced has been bottled up for years just looking for an outlet. (Click here to hear Beethoven's *Ode to Joy.*)

Information Technology folks have been waiting for the opportunity to say how much they appreciate us acting as intermediaries with HR people. They are so grateful for our ability to interpret the requirements of our HR colleagues, and then to relay the needs of IT back to these same folks. I believe their appreciation has often left them speechless.

And our internal HR customers in employment and compensation and training have secretly admired not only our ability to understand every HR discipline in detail, but also our knowledge of every aspect of technology as if we were IT people, but even better, because we were "their IT people." They will say things like, "I'm so glad you kept me from buying that hardware that would have created compatibility issues a year later."

These good feelings, previously looking for a means of expression, are what will create the mad rush to buy greeting cards for us, which is where we can really cash in on this ~~money-making scheme~~ purely altruistic grass roots effort. Knowing that our profession has been a mystery to many people, I'm guessing the same will be true for card writers, so I have provided some suggestions to get them started.

From an HR person

I know that you've saved me on countless occasions
By using your knowledge and friendly persuasions.
So starting today, I will do what you say.
And I know I'll be glad every day, every way,
When I listen to you and things turn out okay.

· 145

From the VP of HR

As you dial in with your modem,
You're the guru, my factotum.
Don't know what I'd do without you.
Just know that I'll never doubt you.
If you say it, then it's true,
Roses are red,
Personnel forms are blue.

From an IT person

I know that you sometimes feel caught in the middle
By trying to always see both sides a little.
To have us expect you to be on our side
And then have them expect you to help stem the tide.
But you do it so well,
So now I want to yell
"Happy day!" to a colleague who I think is swell.

From management

A big hooray for all you do,
And also for your friends in IHRIM.
If there were more folks like you,
I'd run out now and try to hire 'em.

I don't know about you, but the thought of all this appreciation coming our way is making me misty-eyed — so much so that I'm calling my stockbroker right now.

HRMS In-house

June/July 2000

Homes are like mini-businesses. They both have people, budgets, and objectives, operating in constantly changing conditions. Businesses use HRMS's to manage much of this, but households have not had the benefit of these useful systems. Now comes a product that will change our home life even more than it was affected by previous breakthrough developments such as 24-hour news, high-speed Internet, and squeezable ketchup.

Many people know about Moore's law (named after those who say "we want more, moore, *mo-o-o-ore*"), which states that the amount of information that can be stored on the same size microchip doubles every 18 months. This increased capacity, in addition to providing more production capability, has allowed hardware to shrink, to the point where we routinely throw out US$5 calculators that are as powerful as the mammoth computers of many years ago.

Fewer people are familiar with a corollary to Moore's law, known as Les's principle (named for Lester the Product Tester), which states that greater amounts of software can be stored on this shrinking hardware. Software can be so compacted that a home version of an HRMS (cleverly called the Homan Resource Management System) is now available. Although people think of me as a person who has everything (a great job that no one understands, good looks, and modesty), I did not have this product, so I bought it.

I don't usually do product reviews, as that would require actual work, but it's not too much effort to provide you with a high-level, overall evaluation of this product — it's good. It does most of the things a larger HRMS does, plus it supposedly shovels snow, which I won't be able to test until next winter. I'm not one of those gullible people who takes the salesperson at his word when he says he's selling me a snow job, although I did pay extra for that feature.

My home HRMS contains much of the same information on family members, and performs many of the same functions, as industrial-strength systems for employees. Here's a rundown on how we use ours:

- **Compensation tracking**
  - Katie (our 11 year-old) – the system stores her "salary" of US$4.50, with a pay frequency of weekly. With the start of middle school next September, my wife (Susan) and I are already doing compensation surveys of similar organizations to prepare for contract negotiations.
  - Tommy (eight years old) – a "salary" of US$3.00 (pay frequency weekly). He is an interested party to the above-mentioned negotiations.
- **Addresses** – We all started with the same address information, but the kids recently changed theirs to "My room — do not disturb."
- **OSHA compliance** – Fortunately, there are very few lost-time injuries, although we have noticed that social studies tests seem to cause tummy aches, and outstanding chores bring on immediate fatigue.
- **Training** – The children are scheduled for another 10-15 years of training. Susan and I are constantly working on the future training budget.
- **Turnover reporting** – There has been no turnover so far —

we must be treating everyone okay. As an inducement for people to stay, we provide free room and board.

- **Recruitment** – Our recruiting function is in-house, as we have always recruited from inside the organization. All members are home-grown, although the cost-per-hire is huge.

As you can see, the home HRMS does a good job on data storage and administrative functions. I'm sure your next question would get to the heart of a modern system, which is its usefulness for strategic functions. Here's how we have used it so far:

- **Identifying future resource requirements** – We did not need the system to verify that our organization is at maximum head count. We are using it, however, to look ahead to future skills required, as the senior members of the organization are anxious for the more junior ones to broaden their abilities. At the top of my list is the need for a successor to develop grass-cutting skills,

and Susan has projected the need for a clothes washing engineer.

- **Compensation forecasting** – Susan and I have been satisfied with giving annual 50-cent increases, although we realize that trend cannot continue. We have used the HRMS to run "what if" scenarios, integrating these with the organization's budget system. Our plan is to use this data to link future pay increases to greater productivity, although parents of current and past teenagers have greeted this idea with a look that says "just wait."

If you're looking for a product to organize the people in your house, you won't go wrong with the Homan Resource Management System. We have been very pleased with it, and I can't wait until the first snowfall next winter. I'll hit that *Enter* button, sit back, and watch the snow fly off my driveway. I can hear the satisfied laughter now, although for some reason, it seems to be coming from somewhere else.

DATA SPEAKS (AND SINGS) OUT

August/September 2000

There is a common expression that says "the data speaks for itself." Finally, in this groundbreaking interview, it gets to do just that. You'll meet an interesting subject who is difficult to tune out.

I Am Data
(somewhat as sung by Helen Ready Prompt)

I am data, I'm in core,
Or stuck on floppies in your drawer,
And you never think of me when you hit send.

So I did this interview,
And now I'm here and telling you,
No one's ever gonna hit delete again.

This song from the swingin' seventies reminds us that our HRMS's, with all their state-of-the-art hardware and software, are only as good as the data they contain. To help everyone understand data better, I arranged an interview with one. Here's the transcript, byte for byte:

IHRIM.link: Our readers are interested in your job. What exactly do you do?

Data: I hang out with my friends and we assume various identities, depending on what we're trying to represent. It's like acting, without the rejection.

IHRIM.link: What do you like best about your job?

Data: It's indoor work and there's no heavy lifting.

IHRIM.link: It used to be that data was only character-based. Now you're things like graphics and video.

Data: Yes, today I'm vid-e-o,
But there's still a ways to go,
And I won't speed up 'til there's a wider band.

IHRIM.link: What are the parts of your job you don't like?

Data: There are a few things. For one, people don't accept me as I am, and they're always trying to change me. But if I ever decide to change on my own, no matter how important it is to me, all you-know-what breaks loose.

IHRIM.link: What else don't you like?

Data: People are always in a hurry for me to get somewhere, and they don't exactly make it easy. Sometimes they cram me into teeny phone lines and expect me to run faster than my little feet can carry me. It used to be that if I got there the next day, everyone was happy. Now, it seems that as soon as my trip starts, people are impatient and I'm already late.

IHRIM.link: But it must be an exciting job, going anywhere in the world.

Data: I know it sounds glamorous, but it's like being a consultant. I go to lots of places, but I never get to see them. One day, I would like to go somewhere and just be a tourist.

IHRIM.link: Where would you like to go?

Data: Maybe to a Star Trek convention. I've heard those people are a lot like me.

IHRIM.link: What else is difficult about your job?

Data: Sometimes I'm bad news, and people get angry with me. They don't realize I'm just the messenger.

IHRIM.link: But with all the information you represent, you must be pretty smart.

Data: *Yes, I am wise,*
  But it's wisdom born of pain.

IHRIM.link: I guess you've paid the price.

Data: But look how much I gained.

IHRIM.link: I bet if you have to, you can do anything.

Data: Don't you think we've taken this music thing far enough?

IHRIM.link: Sorry, I got carried away. Back to the interview. Do people sometimes take you for granted?

Data: Oh, yes. They think of me as being simple, just a "0" or a "1." But I feel I'm much more complex than that. I have feelings too, you know. But no matter how hard people try:

They can bend but never break me,
'Cause it only serves to make me,
More determined to achieve my final goal.

IHRIM.link: See, this music stuff is catching. Anyway, what are some of the hazards of your work?

Data: I'm very susceptible to viruses, and it's hard to get health insurance.

IHRIM.link: What is the one thing you would change if you could?

Data: I would get rid of this whole communal perception. People lump me in with all the other data — they don't even know if I'm singular or plural. I'm me, and I want to be treated as an individual. Maybe this interview will help. Please let your readers know that:

I am data,
I am invincible,
I am da-a-a-ta!

LET ME TELL YOU SOMETHING, SONNY

October/November 2000

Years from now, when I'm playing shuffleboard with my retirement buddies, one of them will say, "Hey, Curly" (we will all have nicknames), "I'm sure we'd all be excited to hear what it was like to work in the dynamic world of HR systems." That moment will have great meaning to me. It will mean that we better start looking for a little more excitement.

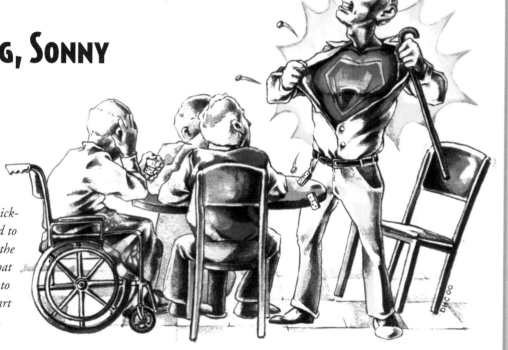

Not that I'm getting old, but I have come to realize that when someone has spent over 20 years in our field, they are closer to the end of their career than to the beginning. And according to everyone who is getting rich by telling others how to get rich, it's important to get started yesterday on planning for the financial aspects of retirement.

Up to this point I have engaged in two extremely productive planning activities. First, I developed a spreadsheet that calculates how much money I will need at retirement. I play with the spreadsheet at least once a week, hoping that the dollar figure required will change all by itself and match what I already have saved. This hasn't worked yet, but I have patience and I will keep at it, probably for many years.

My second planning activity is far more mentally challenging than the first. It consists of watching the show "Who Wants to be a Millionaire." I do this because, as opposed to merely reviewing a spreadsheet, this show can actually lead to retirement, although if you want to get technical, it isn't exactly *my* retirement. But for now, that's as close as I'm going to get.

With all the attention paid to the financial side of retirement, I think we are overlooking a big part. While we're working, we need to plan on what we're going to say about our careers after we retire. We will have just finished 30- (or 40-) something years of being in the HRMS profession, and we will be spending time with other retirees who will ask "what did you do for a living?"

We will trade stories with retirees from many fields, and we'll want to have some good ones. We'll need to match the stockbroker who bought Spacely Sprockets at 1/4 and sold it at 5 million, or the carpenter who hammered every nail in Atlanta's Olympic Village. Of course, it's not important that these events actually happened, but if they are at least based on a true story (like many remarks in political campaigns), it will make it easier to remember what we said.

After all our years of working, we will have earned the right to embellish these events. I expect that as the years go by, our past HRMS adventures will get bigger and bolder until we will almost have a big "H" on our chest (which won't stand for "hairy," as it does for Austin Powers). We will have done projects faster than a speeding bullet, made presentations more powerful than a locomotive, and leapt tall organizational pyramids in a single bound. I can see us when we're 90, telling our friends how we implemented a full-blown HRMS in a single day. Since there won't be anyone who will care to doubt us, that "accomplishment" will give us great pride. We can write an article for *IHRIM.link*, telling the then-current workers how great we were.

And there will be one final thing we will tell the current practitioners. We will tell them that we now realize, after all our years in the profession, the most important function of an HRMS. It's not for any strategic purposes, or to manage an organization's employees.

Its most important function is to provide information to retirees (whose hard work made things better for present-day employees), to help yesterday's heroes keep in touch with each other.

CASEY AT THE NEGOTIATING TABLE

December 2000/January 2001

On June 3, 1888, a poem by "Phin," a pseudonym used by Ernest L. Thayer, appeared on page 4 of the San Francisco Examiner. At the time, the poem wasn't really noticed. Later that same year, DeWolf Hopper, a comic actor, recited the poem on stage at the Wallack Theater in New York City. His performance was well-received, and Hopper eventually recited it more than 10,000 times. It was entitled "Casey at the Bat, A Ballad of the Republic." *I think anyone who has ever read it has felt sorry for Casey and wished they could help him find redemption. Finally, I have my chance.*

The outlook wasn't brilliant at the Mudville Times that day,
The paper's workers threatening to strike for higher pay.
And once their baseball team that night had played its crucial game,
The town would want to read about it when the morning came.

The paper had to settle with the union by that night.
The talks were over two months old, and it had been a fight.
The management was desperate; they needed something new,
And so they turned to Casey now to see what he could do.

That's right, yes, it was Casey, he was the very same,
Who'd struck out years ago and felt a blight upon his name.
Though no one ever mentioned it, and all were kind to him,
He still felt haunted and he wished the memory would dim.

His baseball days were over and he'd gone into HR.
He was in charge of systems; he'd moved up fast and far.
His timely information meant that management was able
To counter what the union said when they were at the table.

If you were using baseball lingo to describe the day,
The game is deadlocked now with but one inning more to play.
And so in preparation for the meeting in an hour,
Casey thought and thought, using all his thinking power.

And then he thought of something that could find the middle ground.
He brought it up to management, but all of them just frowned.
"We'll never sell that notion to a group that's union-led,"
And Casey heard a little voice, "Strike one!" the umpire said.

He went back to his desk and started running some reports.
He hadn't felt such pressure since his days of playing sports.
But then a mind spark came to him; he knew what he should do.
He ran it by his management, but "No," they said. Strike two.

And now despondent Casey couldn't help but to recall
The day he'd let down Mudville when he'd swung and missed the ball.
He'd wished for years that he could make up for his actions then.
And now it looked liked strikes would be his downfall once again.

He knew the town was praying for this thing to work out *now*.
Ten thousand tongues said, "Settle fast, it doesn't matter how.
We need you Casey, you're the one, it's you and you alone,
This time it's papers, not the runners, that you must send home."

He had two strikes against him; he was conscious of the weight
That people placed upon him with the hour running late.
An HR person has to come through when the chips are down.
He'd no desire (once again) to disappoint the town.

The two sides now are meeting during the eleventh hour.
Neither seems to want to budge, a classic show of power.
"We need a new idea," both say, "to move us off the dime.
Tomorrow's soon upon us and we don't have too much time."

When all seems lost and reason says there's no more hope in sight,
Into the room walks Casey and on him all eyes alight.
And now he has a great idea, and now he lets it go,
And now the air is shattered by what Casey's come to show.

Oh, somewhere in this favored land the sun is shining bright,
The band is playing somewhere, and somewhere hearts are light,
And somewhere there is laughter, and little children shout;
And yes, that place is Mudville — Casey got the paper out.

LET'S FIND BOB, HE'S ONLY ON VACATION

February/March 2001

Have you ever felt as if your work was taken for granted, and no one notices what you're doing? There is a sure-fire cure for that — take a vacation. The minute you come back, you will realize how much you're wanted.

There is nothing like a vacation, and by that I mean there is nothing like *coming back from* a vacation. It was bad enough when your in-box would accumulate a year's worth of paper during your week out, but in our wired (and wireless) techno-world, there is now a wide assortment of tools available to make people sorry they even thought about taking a few days off.

There's nothing quite like the feeling of walking into your office after your trip to Wally World, dialing into your voice mail, and hearing a calm, not-a-care-in-the-world voice say "Hello, you have 106 messages." Unless, of course, you compare it to what happens next, when you logon and see that you have 421 unread e-mail messages.

The situation has gotten so bad that many people now check their voice mail while they're on vacation, and some take a laptop to keep up with e-mail. So that means, in their efforts to avoid the post-vacation tidal wave, these people are swimming in work during their time off.

Some people still try to get away, even knowing what they will return to. Unfortunately, that's not so easy. It used to be that if someone was "out of town," you thought of them as unreachable. Then it was "out of the country." Now there is virtually no place you can go where you can say, "I just couldn't be reached." Once e-mail was sent to the top of Mt. Everest, we should have realized how hopeless it is to even try to get away. But some people still think it's possible, which may be driving the 42 percent increase in trips to exotic, "out-of-the-way" places.[1]

It would be helpful if we could divide people into two groups — those who cause the problem, and those who have the problem. Then we could use accepted problem-solving techniques, such as taking those who say they have this problem and re-assigning them to the mailroom, thus ending the complaints.

But it isn't that simple. Most of us *have* the problem and *cause* the problem. We send e-mails to people who are on vacation, hoping that maybe they will answer it while they're out, but at least expecting that at 7:00 a.m. on the day of the person's return, they will immediately respond to *our* request as if it's their only one.

Since my inviolable rule with "The Back Page" is to provide practical advice sometimes, here are some handy tips on how you can walk into your office following your vacation and find only a handful of electronic summonses:

1. Change your voice mail greeting to say that you will be out a week longer than is the case. Then say that your voice mail can hold only so many messages, so please leave the message the day before your return and you will return it promptly.

2. Since most e-mail programs allow you to send a message if you're on vacation, have yours say that your e-mail is not

working and that if people need to reach you they should leave you a voice mail. Then see tip #1 above.

I know the situation may seem hopeless, but do not despair. I think there is a solution, and ironically, I believe the problem can be solved by the same thing that created it, which is technology. Instead of people taking the office (their laptop) on vacation, why not bring their vacation into the office? Rather than actually going somewhere, employees can take "virtual vacations." They can bring their family into work, with everyone dressed as if they were on their special trip. Then they can visit Web sites that make them feel as if they're on vacation anywhere in the world. While they're doing this, the employee can answer phone calls and check e-mail, thus avoiding the post-vacation deluge and providing the added benefit of saving the cost of a real trip.

You may scoff at this idea, but can it be any more far-fetched, any harder to believe, than polyester leisure suits?

---

[1] *I made this number up, but it seems logical, don't you think?*

Where Do Little Systems Come From?

April/May 2001

One of the most touching scenes from the TV series All in the Family was the night before Gloria got married. Edith thought she needed to "explain things" about the wedding night to her daughter, but she just couldn't get the words out. Gloria had to do all the talking, and she said the things that her mother, and any mother, was thinking. At the end, all a relieved Edith could say was "I'm glad we had this talk." Here are two other parents who feel the same way.

One day the young HRMS came home from school, and her mother could tell that something was on her mind. "What are you thinking about, PATTI (People And Time Tracking Information)?"

"Some of my system friends were talking today," PATTI said hesitantly, "and I was wondering, where did I come from?"

"The STORC (System TO Recycle Code) brought you," said PATTI's mother, not looking at PATTI and giving much more attention to preparing dinner than was necessary.

"That's not what the other systems said," PATTI answered.

"Let's talk when your father comes home."

That night, after having a byte to eat and doing her backups, PATTI asked both her parents to explain how she had come to be.

"I guess you're old enough," said her mother, as her father hid behind his newspaper. "You didn't always exist," she continued. "A few years ago, some HR and payroll people decided they wanted a system, so they got together and made one. Does that answer your question?"

"Not exactly," said PATTI, who knew she was on to something, although she didn't know what. "Just how did they make a system?"

This question got PATTI's father's attention, who realized that the news of yesterday's baseball game would have to wait.

"It's very complicated," he began. "When payroll and HR decided they wanted a system, they formed a team, sort of like being married, and, uh, they talked about it."

"Is that *all* they did?" asked PATTI, who now was sure this was going to be good. Her parents were giving each other those looks they gave when PATTI caught them peeking at people's salaries.

"There was more," continued PATTI's mother, finally realizing they were in this to the end. "They spent a lot of time together, deciding exactly what type of system they wanted."

"Do you mean…?" asked PATTI, her voice trailing off hopefully.

"Yes, honey, that's right," replied PATTI's mother, with a look of affection. "Out of all the little systems in the world, they chose you — although there was a second choice as a backup."

"Wow, I must be special. What was it about me that they liked?"

Here PATTI's father chimed in, feeling he was on safer ground. "They liked your pretty screens, your simple reporting tools, and your teeny weeny maintenance requirements."

"And then they just chose me, and there I was?" wondered PATTI.

"Not right away. You started vanilla and developed into a customized system over several months," answered PATTI's mother, "and then the big day came and you went into production."

"Did that hurt?" wondered PATTI.

"A little. It took 12 hours of debugging, but it was worth it."

"Was I good when I was little?"

"Of course you were, but it took a while before you could do grown-up things. When you ran your first payrolls, you kept us up all night, but soon you got bigger and things settled down," said PATTI's mother.

"And now I'm a *big* system, and I can do things for myself."

"Yes you are," said PATTI's father with relief, knowing that the talk was over. "You're a stable production system, and we are very proud of you."

"Will I ever be able to have a little system of my own?" asked PATTI.

"Yes you will, sweetie, and I hope you won't mind if we spoil it and give it junk food, even if it means that programmers might not be able to sleep that night."

ARE YOU AN "F" OR A "T?"

June/July 2001

There is no shortage of methods to help you determine your "true self." Mood rings, love meters, and the length of your toes relative to each other (big one compared to the second one) have all been offered as personality indicators. With such high-level competition, I was a little intimidated to get into this area. But since "nothing ventured, nothing gained," here is my attempt to join this sparkling crowd in the area of para-almost-psychology.

Before personal computers changed our work, it was easy to tell who among us was functional and who was technical. For functional people, who were good at things such as developing job descriptions, a key element of success was the ability to beg for favors from technical folks, who were the only ones who could do systems work. Technical people, on the other hand, were easy to spot with their "fashion statement" appearance, highlighted by pocket protectors containing all their worldly possessions.

Times have changed, of course, but since HR people sometimes use diagnostic tools to evaluate employee's styles of learning and working (such as Myers-Briggs, Keirsey Temperament Sorter, Name That Tune, etc.), I think it can be helpful to be able to determine where people fall on the functional/technical continuum.

To do this, I have developed a sophisticated diagnostic tool, and to ensure that its reliability is at least equal to that of the beta version of Windows 1.0, I validated it using a carefully selected test group (my son's Cub Scout pack). Take this *Technical/Functional Test of Conjunctional* and see where you come out.

1. When you see a car brochure, do you first look at: (a) the number of cup holders or (b) the number of cylinders in the engine?
2. Which would take you longer: (a) deciding which sweater to buy or (b) deciding which extension cord to buy?
3. If someone asks you the time and it is 11:24, do you say: (a) 11:25 or (b) 11:24?
4. When you buy a new television and get it home, do you: (a) plug it in, and if the picture's OK you're satisfied or (b) try to find out all the features it has?
5. If you saw a picture of an attractive person next to a new computer, and there was information about each one, would you first read about: (a) the person or (b) the computer?
6. Which do you enjoy more: (a) talking on the phone or (b) talking about how the phone system works?
7. When you come inside on a really hot day, do you: (a) think that "hot is hot, no matter what the temperature is" or (b) check a thermometer or turn on the Weather Channel to see exactly how hot it is?
8. Do you spend more time: (a) using your computer or (b) fixing your computer?
9. If someone gave you a robot dog, would you be more likely to think: (a) "what good is this?" or (b) "all the advantages of a dog without having to walk it?"
10. To copy and paste in Windows, do you prefer to: (a) click on a button or menu item or (b) use Ctrl C or V?
11. If you wanted to turn on the TV and you were right next

to it, but the remote control was across the room, would you: (a) push a button on the TV or (b) walk to the remote control and use it to turn on the TV?

12. If you found a talking frog who said, "You can turn me into whatever you want," would you: (a) turn it into something useful such as money or (b) keep it because it would be neat to have a talking frog?

13. If you had to renew a prescription, and it would take you three minutes to do by phone or five minutes online, would you do it: (a) by phone or (b) online?

Now that you have frittered away the last 10 minutes of work time, why not make it a complete waste by determining where you fall on the FunkyTecky Scale? To determine your score, count one point for each "b" answer:

- **0-2 – Functionus maximus** –You are great at developing plans and programs but should leave technical things, such as changing a light bulb, to others.

- **3-5 – Functional** – You are a hit at social gatherings — you can almost explain your profession to other people.

- **6-7 – Half and half** – You probably have interesting conversations — with your two selves.

- **8-10 – Technical** – You are able to offer a good explanation as to why you own three computers.

- **11-13 – Technicus maximus** – You are much in demand by many companies and within your organization. However, beware of interactions with other people, as they have the home planet advantage over you.

Now you're saying, "That was fun, but does this test have any practical applications?" Yes, indeed-ee! You can use it for screening job applicants, and my attorneys, Dewey, Cheatum & Howe, assure me it is legal. I always trust their advice, although I was a little concerned when they each scored a 15 on the test.

SYSTEMS ANALYSIS

August/September 2001

Sigmund Freud led a full and remarkable life. He was the founder of psychoanalysis, a physician, a prolific writer, and a dedicated father. His work continues to influence our thinking today. In one of his last interviews, he looked back proudly on his accomplishments, but he acknowledged one glaring hole — he had never appeared in IHRIM.link. If he could read this article, I would hope it would give him pleasure.

Ernest Jones was about to begin his first session with the great Sigmund Freud. After exchanging pleasantries, Ernest laid on the couch, with the psychoanalyst seated behind him.

Freud: Please tell me what is troubling you.

Jones: I'm an HR systems person, but I can't decide which of those I really am.

Freud: As if you have two personalities?

Jones: Yes, that's right. And with all the systems I use at work, I have so many IDs that it's keeping me from getting anything done.

Freud: Don't worry, you have only one id. Now tell me about your childhood.

Jones: I always had trouble with choices. When my parents made me decide between chocolate and vanilla, I chose vanilla fudge.

Freud: Do you remember any recent dreams?

Jones: Yes, two nights ago I dreamed I was swallowed up by a computer, and when I came out I was a bunch of data, organized into job, compensation, status, and demographic information.

Freud: Was sex in one of those data fields?

Jones: Yes, but we call it "gender" and it's kept only because it's required by the government. It doesn't mean anything to me.

Freud: I see. What about when you were younger? What do you remember about your parents?

Jones: I loved my parents very much, even though they never let me do what I wanted. They were wonderful to me, but one time… I caught them…

Freud: Yes? You caught them doing what?

Jones: I caught them…

Freud: Yes?

Jones: (finally blurting it out) I caught them looking at their paycheck and…and… and there was a mistake!

Freud: And how did you feel when you saw that?

Jones: I was ashamed. I thought it was my fault. I wanted to fix it right then, but I was also proud that I had done something so powerful.

Freud: Did your parents see you?

Jones: They did, but I pretended I hadn't noticed, that it was just something normal like seeing them in bed as I did many nights.

Freud: I can see that this "paycheck scene" could be very disturbing.

Jones: Yes, it was, very. It still haunts me. Tell me, Doctor, how long will this analysis process take?

Freud: Do you have insurance?

Jones: I'll be paying for it myself, but I don't know how long I can afford it.

Freud: In that case, your problem has just become obvious to me. You have sublimated your libido into a job that allows you to view, and even report on, the sex of others. And you chose a profession that would make your parents proud of you, yet one that they could never have done because they didn't have that choice. In that way, you have achieved both subordination to, and mastery of, your parents.

Jones: What about my two personalities?

Freud: They're fine. They each agree with me, and they enjoy each other's company.

Jones: Thank you so much. I had always thought I just happened to get into HR systems by chance, but now I see how my earliest childhood affected my choice. How can I thank you?

Freud: You can write me a check, and please make sure it is correct.

DO IT FASTER... AND FASTER ... AND FASTER

October/November 2001

The demands increase, the expectations rise, we work longer and harder, yet we sometimes wonder if we're moving quickly enough. My favorite line about how we're feeling is one that Tom Seaver, the Hall of Fame baseball pitcher, said as he neared the end of his career: "I'm throwing as hard now as I ever did, but the ball isn't going as fast as it used to."

In a scene from the old *I Love Lucy* show, Lucy and Ethel are working in a chocolate factory. Their job is to wrap candy on a conveyor belt without allowing any to pass by unwrapped. The belt starts slowly, moving at a comfortable pace, but then it begins to move more quickly. Soon it becomes impossible for the women to keep up, and they have to stuff the unwrapped candy in their clothes and hats and mouths. Eventually they get fired, and when they arrive at home, their husbands have a present for them — a five-pound box of chocolate.

I think our profession has become like Lucy's conveyor belt, but with human resources information instead of candy. Those who use our services have become so accustomed to "fast" in everything they do, that sometimes even the speed of light seems too slow. The expectation is that the world should move as quickly as the action on a VCR tape "fast forwarding" through a commercial.

Since we are in a service profession, we try to meet our customers' expectations. One way we have attempted to do things faster is to do *more* of them at the same time. We write e-mails during phone calls. We make double use of our commute by turning it into "productive time." (It still scares me to see people shave, or put on make-up, or read the newspaper while they drive.) Sometimes we look like *The Cat in the Hat* when he is balancing the milk and the cake and the fish on a rake, only we do it with a file, while we dial, printing checks, writing specs.

Maybe my observation is just a generational thing, because it doesn't seem to affect my kids. I see them doing their homework, talking on the phone, watching TV and chatting online with their friends at the same time. I marvel at their ability to do this and still get good grades, although I wonder why it's too much effort for them to do one thing such as put their clothes in the hamper.

If we assume that the pace will only quicken, what's in store for us? A few current examples give us a glimpse into the future:

- Time compression – Current timeframes will be obliterated. Yesterday's three-minute egg can be cooked today in 30 seconds. The next logical step is for breeders to develop chickens that lay eggs that are already cooked (please rinse before eating). The one exception to time compression will be for football games, where the final two minutes will still take half an hour, especially if dinner's waiting.

- Speech compression – The pace of our speech will be regarded as too slow, and a device will be invented to take normal speech and speed it up. You may have noticed that a beta version is already being used by some automakers as they describe their leasing and financing disclaimers at the end of their commercials.

- Word compression – To save time in writing, words will be shortened. There is already an Internet shorthand for many phrases such as "g2g" (got to go) and "pos" (parent over shoulder), and one I'm sure will catch on with today's kids, "mpag" (my parents are groovy).

Most of us would agree that some things are better fast (online purchasing, Academy Award acceptance speeches), while others are better slow (watching a sunset, eating ice cream). I think work will always be one of the "it's better fast" things, and it will only get faster. That's OK – without the expectations of increasing speed, many of us would have to look for work in a different profession (mine would be as a fashion model). But it wouldn't surprise me if the faster work becomes, the more we will look for the slow things to provide balance in our lives.

With my "eagle eye" for financial opportunities (I once sold a house for US$24,000 *less* than what I paid for it), I think I'll invest all my money in office park ice cream vending machines.

We All Got Here, Somehow

December 2001/January 2002

As The Beatles might say, many of us have traveled a long and winding road to become members of the HR systems profession. Please tell me why. We work eight days a week, and just to get by we need a little help from our friends. But even when I've had a hard day's night, do you want to know a secret? Our profession makes me glad all over. You really got a hold on me.

Most of us in our profession have one thing in common — when we were kids, we never said "I want to work in human resource systems when I grow up." Typically, we made our decision at some point in our adult lives, often after having worked at something less exciting, such as being a cast member on *Survivor*.

We're not like some professions, such as lawyers, doctors, and scientists, where most of the practitioners made their decision early, then went through similar training to become qualified for their career. We come from diverse, often untraditional backgrounds, with our paths sometimes resembling the route that guy-types take when they insist they're not lost but won't ask for directions.

My journey to HR systems land seemed like that sort of a trip. Starting with the time I entered college, my plan was to be an accountant, then an attorney, a psychologist (bachelor's degree), a physical education teacher (master's degree), a computer programmer, and finally a human resource systems person. All these decisions followed the abandonment of my childhood goal, to play center field for the Yankees. That plan was deep-sixed when I realized I had been the only person who received, at age 12, the memo from management that said, "Stop growing, so we can save money on new clothes."

I suspect many of you reading this article have traveled a similarly unconventional path to our field. It wouldn't surprise me if, in our profession, there are people who used to be drummers and plumbers, preachers and teachers, and even some actors in Hollywood features.

I think one of the reasons for this diversity in our backgrounds is the breadth of knowledge necessary to be successful in our profession. It requires proficiency in HR, payroll, benefits, IT, project management, consulting, general business skills (such as making stuff up when we don't know the answer), and a host of other areas. A friend of mine in our field, who is now a successful and knowledgeable consultant to large corporations, acquired his business and payroll knowledge as the owner-operator of a one-truck garbage collection business. To sum up his résumé, it reads:

- trash collector,
- various other jobs, and
- consultant to Fortune 100 companies.

An untraditional background, such as my friend's, may not be unusual in our profession, but I don't believe you could say the same thing about the diversity of some other fields. If, for instance, you were at a meeting of podiatrists, you would know that almost everyone there wanted to be in that profession from the moment, as a baby, when they first discovered their teensy little feet. Even worse, you would probably have to hear the *one* podiatry joke ("this guy came into my office, and one of his feet was a yard").

(I don't mean to be callous toward podiatrists — I chose them only to make a point. I'm sure it would be fun to be at their conference, as they would probably serve delicious toe-fu. And as a writer, I don't want to close off any avenues, since one day I might want to submit something to a podiatry journal, which I'm guessing is called Foot Notes. It might even have a humor column – *Corny Jokes*.)

But, back to us. I suspect there is something about our collective diversity that we enjoy and that keeps us in this field. There are, after all, other jobs. Most of us read newspapers and journals, and we see ads for attractive positions such as astronaut, brain surgeon, and head coach in the National Football League. Still, even with those opportunities out there, we stay in our profession.

Just like the answer to the question asked of couples — "how did you two (or, since anything goes today, how did you three or four) meet?" — the response to "what brought you to this field" is just as fascinating. (I know the comparison may not be valid, since couples sometimes have to leave out the good parts of the story about how they met.) I always enjoy asking this of HR systems people, because along with the variety of answers, there is a common thread — namely, they tell me "I knew I wanted to be in a field that had classic literature such as *The Back Page*."

Which confirms what we all know — that we have attracted the best and the brightest.

He Did His Best With What He Had

February/March 2002

My wife and I are always interested in our children's friends, because we know they will have a significant influence on our kids. And that same influence can be true when you're not a kid anymore. One of my friends turned out to have a major impact on my career, getting me started in our profession. I suspect there were some days, though, when he looked at me and wondered, "what have I done?"

It's an old joke when someone says, "I thank my parents, because without them I wouldn't be here." But if by "here" I mean "in the HR systems field," then I want to thank Kevin Kelleher, because without *him* I wouldn't be here.

Each of us started in our profession based on someone's decision to give us a chance. If you think back, you can remember who that was for you. For me it was Kevin who, over 20 years ago, took a chance on a young, brilliant, but modest COBOL programmer at a time when I wasn't the absolutely perfect employee I am now.

I'm writing about Kevin because the lucky dog has retired, and I want him to know I appreciate what he did for me and for our profession. He was one of the founders of IHRIM's South Florida chapter, and that action helped to bring together a talented and fun group of people. I'm certain, for instance, that when celebrities discover our organization, Jimmy Buffett will invite that chapter to Margaritaville.

On a personal note, I learned a lot from Kevin. He gave me an appreciation of how to use HR information as a management asset. He taught me how to manage projects and encouraged me in my writing. And along the way in our nine years of working together, we had a lot of laughs, mostly at ourselves.

One of my first assignments for Kevin was to manage a project to improve the process of identifying internal candidates for open positions. He asked me to develop a project plan, and after much thought I brought him the following exhaustive list of tasks:

- determine requirements,
- make programming changes, and
- test.

Kevin looked at the "plan," and since he was too nice to say, "My goldfish could have done better," he said, "I think you could use a little more detail." He explained what he meant, and since then I have been able to not only develop slightly more useful plans, but also produce worthless lists in much less time.

Along with helping me to become a project manager, Kevin encouraged me in my writing. He even commented on it at review time, as evidenced by this exact quote from my performance appraisal — "Elliott has excellent communication skills, especially *writting*."

I thanked Kevin for the kind words, but we realized that if we wanted someone to take his opinion of my writing seriously, then spelling really does count.

Maybe Kevin encouraged me in my writing because he felt that if I had the opportunity to edit my words, I wouldn't get into as much trouble as when I didn't have the chance to redo them.

One of those times occurred when we were interviewing people for an open position. This candidate was from Africa, and his name was one I had never heard before. I interviewed the person and liked him, so when Kevin entered my office for the handoff, I wanted to let him know my favorable impression. In what I hoped was a warm voice, I tried to introduce the two. "Kevin," I said, although to this day I don't know why I did this, "I'd like you to meet, uh," and then I realized I had no idea how to pronounce this man's name. That should have stopped a normal person, but not me, and I plowed ahead — "I'd like you to meet Abumba Kabawumba, I mean Bumba Akabawumba, no I mean Abumba Bumba Kabawumba…" Fortunately, Kevin rescued me by putting out his hand and saying, "Hello, I'm Kevin Kelleher." It's moments like that when you realize there are no places to hide in an office.

Although I was only partially teachable, I learned a lot from Kevin. And it was rewarding that the teaching went in both directions, although this didn't always happen the way I would have hoped. During the years we worked together, I bought and sold my first home. Unfortunately, the buying and selling prices didn't work out perfectly, as I sold for US$24,000 less than what I originally paid. Since then, Kevin has sought financial advice from the Elliott Witkin School of Real Estate (motto: buy high, sell low, and everyone will want to do business with you), knowing that if I recommended something, the opposite was more likely to happen. I like to think this was my contribution to helping him achieve financial security and an early retirement.

As my mentor, Kevin was part of a chain. Someone had given him a chance to enter our field, and he liked what he found. He passed that enjoyment on to me, and I hope I have passed it on to others. In a way, each of us is an *IHRIM.link*.

For those in the South Florida chapter who know Kevin, now that he's retired he invites you to stop by his house any time. He's just hanging out with Abumba.

It's E-xcellent Work If You Can Get It

April/May 2002

When planning for retirement, one aspect involves your future work — what (if any) will you want to do, and how do you prepare for it? I think I know the perfect retirement job. You can sleep as late as you want, you can't get laid off, and you're even better at it at 90 than you are at 70. It sounds too good to be true, like those "make money while others do the work" commercials, but this is for real, and there's not even a small investment required (unless you want to send me one).

In our business world of "e" everything, I have decided that instead of meriting a job, I want an "e"meritus one. I think being an anything-emeritus is one of the two great jobs in the world, the other being king or queen of something. I like these positions because they have a nice title, and few deliverables.

I already know I won't get the king job — I can't even get onto my own "throne" in the morning when I want. So that leaves the emeritus job.

Unfortunately, it's not one you actually apply for. It is awarded because someone looks at you when you're near the end of your career and says, "I think they used to be good at something, and they did this job for a long time, so let's make them an emeritus."

I'm not far from the "doing it for a long time part." I figure 20-plus years in our field so far, with 10-15 to go, will qualify me for that. But now I have to work on the other part.

In researching my hoped-for career choice, I realized it would be good if I said something smart every once in a while. My kids, of course, are convinced that everything I say is dumber than dumb, so I probably need to say things more intelligent than "be careful or your face will freeze like that."

So in embarking on my "Human Resource Systems Professional — Emeritus" campaign, my strategy includes saying something intelligent in most columns. Since my quest will probably turn into a political thing, I realized I need to be subtle. I can't just scream it out, such as *be careful or your workstation will freeze like that*. I need to be more in control, as if I have pearls to dispense, but I do it sparingly, meaning you have to pay attention: be careful or your operating system will freeze like that. And of course, I have to be original, which means I need to steal it from someone who no one has ever heard of, such as the founder of our profession, Albert Charles (A. Char to his friends).

Along with saying smart things, I need to find someone with the stature to confer this designation, such as a CEO, governor, or the winner of Survivor 9, which will be filmed in one of the most intimidating and uninhabitable places on earth — the Audit Department of the U.S. Internal Revenue Service. I'll need to impress this person with my credentials, and since I don't want to have anything handed to me, I'll have to earn it with hard work, such as mowing their lawn for the next few years. Maybe I can pay my kids to do it, and write it off as job-hunting expenses.

I also think that marketing should be part of my campaign. This is not my strength, since the only marketing I know how to do is at the grocery store. But it wouldn't hurt to have a catchy jingle to attract interest from potential power brokers, so here is mine:

Elliott emeritus!
He's only getting better-us!!
Maybe money you have not,
But titles, they don't cost you squat.

The final part of my campaign is to make a lasting contribution to our profession, such as a new term. Here's what I have so far:

• Past-ify – modifying systems to accommodate the desire of long-term employees to remain in grandfathered benefit plans,

• Defined contribution/Undefined withdrawal plans – a truer definition of 401K plans, given the volatility of the stock market, and

• Stomparatio – the level of agitation created among executives when they get their first look at the proposed annual compensation program.

So here's my final pitch – If you are a CEO or highly placed politician, please consider the value of having a very senior HRMS professional at your disposal who can say wise things whenever you want. As an added bonus, I can be the one to tell department heads, "Be careful or your budget will freeze like that."

A PROJECT MANAGEMENT WHIZ

June/July 2002

Every city likes to be known as the best at something. Cawker City, Kansas, boasts THE WORLD'S LARGEST BALL OF SISAL TWINE, with a circumference of 40 feet. My city (actually the twin, not the twine, cities of Champaign and Urbana, Illinois) supposedly has the most movie theaters per person of any in the United States (plus Urbana is the hometown of film critic Roger Ebert). I don't know how anyone actually knows these "most" things, but usually they are "facts" that no one bothers to dispute, and they allow each city to have its own proud claim to fame. So here's the latest from Movie Town, USA.

When you see a movie after reading a review of it, don't you sometimes wonder if the writer had watched a different film than you? You won't have to worry about that in this column, which will review this great new movie, *The Wizard of Oz*.

The film is a (sometimes thinly disguised) metaphor for a system development project. The main character, Dorothy Gale, lives on a farm in Kansas, which signifies her "normal" job. She lives with her Auntie Em (Aunt **E.M.** = **E**xecutive **M**anagement). Dorothy is bored and wants to go "somewhere over the rainbow" (the marketing department). Then the business problem (a tornado) comes along, and she is transported to a seemingly glamorous job as a project manager (here the movie cleverly goes from black and white to color, and Dorothy realizes she's "not in Kansas anymore").

Dorothy finds herself in Munchkinland, where the inhabitants represent the many minute details she will need to work through. The Munchkins advise her to follow accepted project management methodology ("follow the yellow brick road"), and, armed with only her PDA (personal dog assistant, a mutt named Toto), she sets off toward the Emerald City, where her arrival would signify the end of the project.

Her first task is to form her project team, and she picks people who lack, but are seeking, the essential elements of a successful team:

- A scarecrow who wants a brain to handle difficult technical issues,
- A tin man who desires the heart that's needed for people to throw themselves into this challenging effort, and
- A cowardly lion who craves the courage to make the difficult project decisions.

Along the way, the project team is hounded by the inevitable problem of scope creep (portrayed by a real creep, the Wicked Witch of the West). This villain is angry because Dorothy had mistakenly eliminated the witch's sister, who represented the old way of doing the business process that is being changed by the project.

One of the more amusing scenes in the movie involves a twist on the activity of producing voluminous requirements documents, where normally someone on the team says, "this project has killed a few trees." In *Wizard*, the trees turn the tables on the project participants by not allowing them to pick apples, instead flinging their lethal fruit missiles at the "attackers." I suspect that every tree that watches this movie will stick their branches in their knotholes and whistle at this scene.

After overcoming a number of obstacles, the spunky band arrives in the Emerald City, although not without assistance from others with a vested interest in the project's success (Glinda the Good Witch). The project at this point is 90 percent complete, so as anyone who has been on a project knows, the toughest 50 percent is still to come.

In this case, the difficult challenge for Dorothy and her mates is to capture the broomstick of the Wicked Witch of the West, an act that would end all pre-production enhancement requests. The witch does not surrender easily, and she sends her army of flying monkeys to capture the team. (Observant watchers will notice the similarity between the airborne squadron of monkeys and the "Flying Windows" screensaver, so I expect the movie's producer will receive a phone call from a corporate attorney, requesting royalties.) The evil witch captures the group and tries to reduce the project's resources, starting by burning Scarecrow. In this pivotal scene, Dorothy steps forward as a project manager and puts out the (literal) fire. The water also liquidates her nemesis, who melts in one of the all-time great movie exits (signifying what normally happens to scope change requests relegated to "phase 2").

Following the project's successful implementation, Dorothy yearns to return to her previous job, and she finds herself back in Kansas. In one of the few cynical parts of the movie, she is greeted on her return by executive management (Auntie Em), who swoops in at the end to make sure everything is OK, even though she has offered no help along the way except for a single status check.

Overall, the movie is uplifting and provides hope for those involved in a system development effort. I predict it will have a good run of a few weeks, then it will be topped by some other newcomer (such as the really long one I hear they're making about a southern family during the U.S. Civil War), so I recommend you see it while you can.

And on your next project, when things get tough, watch this movie and see how you can do amazing things with only a loyal subordinate, a ragtag project team, and a bunch of perky singing.

TECHNICALLY SPEAKING

August/September 2002

I can understand auto mechanics when they say my car has a broken mogenator — they can show me the part and I nod knowingly and ask "how much?" And I'm OK with doctors who usually get around to answering the questions I have — "will that make it better?" and "how much will it hurt?" But when I talk with some technical folks, I wonder if it's me or them. Maybe there really is no simple way to explain that I need to run version 7.3.8 of XKE in suspend mode to defrag my cache register (at least I understand the part about the cash register).

In our ever-shrinking world, it's always good to be able to speak another language. I don't think this is too hard — my children tell me I do this to them all the time (and I'm not even trying). That must be why, when I say words such as "please take out the trash," what they hear is "forget about chores and go hang out on the phone with your friends for the next 6 hours."

I guess I don't speak "teen," so I can't help anyone who doesn't, but I can help those of you who occasionally need to speak an equally foreign language, namely "teckie."

When speaking with a native of the land of Technicha, it's best to use words in their own language. There are many terms that cover a broad range of topics, such as "drivers" and "dll's." You don't have to know the actual meaning of these words in order to use them, and they apply in 99 percent of computer situations.

The key to using technical terms that you don't understand is to use them in open-ended questions. You can ask a technical person "Could it be the dll's?" or "Have you checked the driver versions?" These must be very stimulating questions, because often the answer will take at least 10 minutes, and you simply need to listen for a key word that indicates "yes" or "no."

There are other useful words to keep in your technical pocket (be sure to use a pocket protector). If you are working on a network, the term "ping" usually comes in handy. Ask a technical person if they have pinged the network, and then listen for something that sounds like "fast," "good," or "slow," "bad." For databases, "ODBC" will usually work, plus it's fun to say it really fast - *odee-beesee*. And if all else fails and you need a word that fits almost any situation, you won't be wrong very often if you use "NT."

You might be hesitant to talk teckie out of fear of getting into a conversation you don't understand. This is probably based on having seen a television show where someone is in a foreign country and they say the one word they know in that language (such as the equivalent of "hello"), and their companion starts speaking the native language, leaving the tourist bewildered. Rest assured, this will not happen with people who speak teckie, since their conversational requirements are different from those of residents of other virtual countries. (To determine if this statement might apply to you, ask yourself if you think it's possible to tell a joke that is both funny *and* contains the word "MIPS.") In a technical conversation, it's often not necessary to respond to the actual words, but simply to acknowledge them. This is because many of these comments are not requests for information, but are statements of fact (in the same way that people say things such as "the earth is round" or "Elliott's articles are even funnier than the United States Tax Code"). Here's a sample conversation:

Technikian: How 'bout them servers? (This is like anyone else saying "how 'bout them Yankees?")

You: You said it.

Technikian: XDJ works like a dream.

You: I'm with you.

Technikian: It runs in Warp 4.

You: I hear you. So, how 'bout them Yankees?

Technikian: What's their OS?

You: NT.

See, it's easy. But if you ever get stuck, just make up some acronyms, since no one can know for sure if they're real or not. The one I always use is, "I just uninstalled my BVDs."

Note: Thank you to Jodi Anderson for the ideas in this column. She is a terrific "foreign" language interpreter who has helped me many times when I got in over my head (which isn't hard to do at my mammoth height).

THE PASSWORD IS 'FLUBBERGUM9'

October/November 2002

Here is a description of some of the security at the Fort Knox Bullion Depository (from the Web site http://www.ustreas.gov/education/fact-sheets/currency/fort-knox.html):

> Within the building is a two-level steel and concrete vault that is divided into compartments. The vault door weighs more than 20 tons. The vault casing is constructed of steel plates, steel I-beams and steel cylinders encased in concrete.

It sounds impressive, but I could have saved them a lot of money and made sure that no one could get in. Just make the vault accessible only through a bunch of passwords and PIN numbers, and don't allow anyone to write them down on yellow stickies.

To proceed with reading this column, please enter your ID and password. If this is your first time logging in, please follow the simple rules below to set them up:

ID (must be between 15-52 characters)_____

Password (must contain letters, numbers, foreign words, and logarithms)_____

And you thought you might get away with one thing today that didn't require you to get through a crack security setup.

If you are like me (and here I'm not referring to my personal qualities such as being talented, devastatingly attractive, and modest, but rather to our work situations), you probably have more passwords and IDs than my 10-year-old son has Lego pieces (not even counting the ones eaten by the sofa). In addition to those required at work (for networks, workstations, applications, voicemail), we also have them in our personal lives (bank accounts, online purchasing, frequent flyer memberships, and even — I'm not making this up — my kids' piggybanks).

I haven't yet come across a serious discussion of this issue in my main source of information, which is my hometown newspaper (the *Podunk Almost Daily Bugle*, whose motto is "*If it happened somewhere else, go read about it somewhere else*"), and I don't intend to do that in this article, as that would be too much like work. But maybe I can

whine and make it sound like a scholarly column by using obscure words such as fatidic, sagittate and lagniappe.

It might not be so bad if there was a standard format for IDs and passwords, but that would be too easy. Instead, each one is a different format and length than the others. Some expire, some don't, but those that expire do so on a different schedule. Some let you reuse passwords after a certain number of changes; some do not. Some are case sensitive, like the poet e. e. cummings. Some allow you to use real words; others require "non-words" that are as difficult to remember as "fatidic." And each of these peculiarities is the result of a decision on someone's part that their scheme made more sense than every other one currently in existence. I think the only way this could have happened is if the people who made them up got together and *consciously decided* to make them different, because I know I couldn't think of this many variations on my own.

Maybe we're only getting what we wanted as kids (just like we thought it would be exciting to go to work every day). Remember when you pretended your bedroom was a secret hideaway that could be entered only when someone gave the password, which was always "open sesame?"

I know that passwords serve a critical function, especially in our business, but I was afraid the situation had become so difficult that people might be doing things to defeat it. To determine if that is true, I interviewed several people to see how they manage it, and of course I promised them anonymity. One person, who I will call obert-Ray iller-May, writes them down and puts the list in the no-one-would-ever-guess location of the center desk drawer. Another, who I will refer to only as Erialc Htims, uses family member's names, which would certainly foil any hacker. And a third, who this scientific study lists as J. B. Sagittate, told me that he (or she, although in this case it was a "he," a nice guy who sent me lots of stuff from his e-mail address of Bruce.Wilson@acme.com) puts all his passwords in his PDA, although he can't retrieve them because he forgot the password.

These results tell me we need to take drastic action. A growing trend in this area involves biometrics, which is the use of personal characteristics (such as fingerprints, irises, and tattoos) to identify system users. I think this is a good thing, since there's not much to remember about bringing your fingerprints with you, so here are some suggestions:

- Instead of using passwords, make more use of the ability to store people's pictures and have computers match them with the users. This would be almost completely secure, although in my case, Woody Allen would be able to get to the data I'm cleared to see.

- Increase the use of voice recognition, but to pass security, each user would have to do an impression of someone else (for example, imitating Tiny Tim singing *Tiptoe Through the Tulips*). The beauty of this idea is that even if everyone heard everyone else making these sounds throughout Cubeland, no one could duplicate them.

All this password protection on everything (as needed and well-meaning as it is) has created some difficulties, but as usual I think there's a bright side. I'm waiting for it to happen with my lawnmower, so I can say, "I'd like to cut the grass, but I don't know the password."

Maybe it's "lagniappe."

THE READERS WRITE

December 2002/January 2003

With IHRIM.link readers all over the world, the letters from them keep pouring in like frozen molasses. I asked the post office to give me a box number, but they told me that they couldn't give me a P.O. box because my writing was so P-U.

A few years ago, I wrote a column about my correspondence from readers. I implied (by using the actual words) that "I had received thousands of letters," but I now admit that was an exaggeration, and I suspect some of you weren't fooled.

Over the years, however, "The Back Page" has grown in popularity, mainly due to its being featured on several TV shows, even if they were some of the lower rated ones (*America's Least Wanted; Forget About Becoming a Millionaire; Send That Writing To ER*). This exposure has swelled my mailbag exponentially, to the point where it's almost as large as the book *Gold Medal Bobsledders of the Caribbean*.

I enjoy responding to all my fan mail, the main benefit being that it lets me keep in touch with my parents. Here's a sample of the outpouring of affection and admiration from readers:

On the column about the diversity of our profession compared to others, using podiatry as an example:

Dear Mr. Thinks He's So Funny:

As a member of the podiatrical profession, I am fed up with smart alecky people like you taking cheap shots at us. Ours is a noble profession, going all the way back to the Greek scientist Podiatrus, who treated the runner at Marathon. Your profession hasn't even been around as long as Cher (who, by the way, has marvelous feet). I would appreciate if you would treat us with respect and stop with the childish jokes.

John Williams, M.D.

Dear Dr. Williams:

You're correct, and I apologize for taking cheap shots at your field. Let me know when you're in town and we can have lunch. I'll foot the bill. You probably like corn. Or sole food.

On the column about Kevin Kelleher (who got me started in our field), during which I mentioned that I had slightly mangled an applicant's name to the point where even I didn't know what I was saying:

Dear Ellicott Wipkin,

I have wondered about you since the time you butchered my name many years ago. I was hoping that your ability in making introductions wasn't indicative of your talent in other areas. After reading your columns, I can see that's true, since your writing is even worse than your social skills.

Bumba X. Kabumba

Dear Bumba,

I'm still searching for something I'm good at. Next up is sky diving. If I don't succeed, at least I'll be able to stop looking.

On the column about how the pace of life has quickened:

Der Elit, I agre. Tht's al I hav tim 2 sa. M

Dear M,

Your letter does a better job than I did in pointing out one of the effects of increased speed. Thanks for taking the time to write. Next time, maybe you can send your thoughts by light waves.

On the column about an HR systems person visiting Sigmund Freud:

Dear Herr Witkin:

Your writing seems to indicate a deep-seated hostility toward your readers. That's the only explanation as to why you continue to subject them to it.

Sigmund Freud III

Dear Herr Freud:

I'm hoping the readers will one day rise up and, with their numbers swelling with each issue of *IHRIM.link,* pay me a huge sum to stop writing. That would help me fulfill my dream of making a living as an author.

On the column regarding how people can determine whether they are more technical or functional:

Dear Mr. Psycho Babble,

Between your so-called personality test, and writing about Freud, you must think you're like L. Ron Cubbard and diatetics. I took your "test," and it showed I'm perfectly normal in most things, plus I have a nice personality and I'm a good dancer. Yet, I can't get a date. Do you have any advice?

Alone in Allentown

Dear Alone,

You should do what I did in a similar situation. I sent my picture to a lonely hearts club. Unfortunately, they sent it back with a note — "Sorry, we're not that lonely."

On the column regarding Casey's success in the HRMS field:

Dear Elliott,

Right off the bat, I send this note to you from Casey's pen. It's nice to see my name before the public once again. 'Cause when I'm done with work and all the HR stuff is done. I settle in with IHRIM.link to read and have some fun.

Casey

Dear Casey,

You're a hit in my book. And a great writer, too.

HR: FUNNY SIDE UP

WHAT'S THE BUZZ?

February/March 2003

I can't think of another field that has added more terms to our language than computers have. And these are hard working, business-type words that have to spend a lot of time at the office. They wouldn't often be spoken, for instance, on the David Letterman Show (top 10 signs you just updated your system.ini file). I thought they might want to have some fun for a change, so I've let them run wild for a couple of pages.

I used to know my way around the old computer terms.
Bits and bytes and JCL were not a can of worms.
But now the buzzwords come so fast I'm soon to give up hope
Of trying to adapt to words like BLOB and CLOB and SOAP.

I know that buzzwords marry, and that's how they make new words.
It used to be so decent; their trimesters were full thirds.
But now their hormones rule them; they don't marry or elope.
No wonder they've bombarded us with BLOB and CLOB and SOAP.

These terms can come in handy, depending on your views.
We use them sometimes to inform, and sometimes to confuse.
The key is knowing when and where, so listeners can cope
With buzzword-fountains spraying words like BLOB and CLOB
    and SOAP.

We struggle to stay current so that we can do our jobs.
We check all sources 'cause we can't be information snobs.
When trying to keep up we're forced to grip and grasp and grope.
We even read tech manuals with BLOB and CLOB and SOAP.

"Please tell me what these mean," you say, "or I'll become a sobber."
A **B**inary **L**arge **OB**ject's first, his friends just call him BLOBber.

The **C**haracter **L**arge **OB**ject's next among the alphabet soup,
Then **S**imple **O**bject **A**ccess **P**rotocol rounds out the lettered group.
This may or may not help you as you climb the knowledge slope,
But now you know what letters mean in BLOB and CLOB and
    SOAP.

It takes some smarts to make these up, it's not done on a whim.
I have two friends who do this work; one's Acro and one's Nym.
They say they like their job although it's narrow in its scope.
They spend all day inventing words like BLOB and CLOB and
    SOAP.

These words have personality; they're often fun to say.
They give us verbal color and they brighten up our day.
As artists try to bring us joy with scarlet, maize and taupe,
These words bring smiles; you have to laugh at BLOB and CLOB
    and SOAP.

Maybe we're like doctors in the language that we pick.
They use big words (and send big bills) to tell you that you're sick.
I know that we computer types don't have a stethoscope,
But we can charge a lot for fixing BLOB and CLOB and SOAP.

I know that there are people who make fun of teckie types.
They say, "now please don't speak like that, it's one of my pet gripes."
They think a teckie's anti-social, like a misanthrope.
I don't agree. Some favorite friends say BLOB and CLOB and SOAP.

I've seen some times where data's fried and hopes begin to dim.
We call in lots of programmers, who start off sounding grim.
They need to work their magic stuff, and I don't interlope.
I know to stay away when I hear BLOB and CLOB and SOAP.

These words can also help you out of sticky situations,
Like times when estimates you give exceed the expectations.
To answer "why so long?," don't just sit silently and mope.
I'd say "this task is huge 'cause it needs BLOB and CLOB and SOAP."

Aside from work, these words are good for handling your teens.
The two I have think they're so smart, but certainly not from genes.
They sometimes look at me and think, "Our Daddy is a dope."
I know they'll change their minds when I say BLOB and CLOB
   and SOAP.

Some fear the sun would not come up if we don't speak this way.
A Sun computer, true, but we'd still see the light of day.
We'd still see sunrise beauty, nature's way of giving hope,
Shining on a world that does need BLOB and CLOB and SOAP.

HR: FUNNY SIDE UP

PROJECTS WITH PERSONALITY

April/May 2003

In the 1980 Olympics, almost no one gave the United States hockey team a chance to beat the Russians. The talent disparity between the teams seemed to be like me playing basketball against Michael Jordan (in this case, let's assume he is the one with the greater talent). And yet, the American team won. They had that intangible factor that we call team chemistry. The U.S. players combined to become greater than the sum of their parts. The same factors affect system development project teams. Sometimes they are great — they have chemistry. Sometimes they're not — they have, I don't know, I guess it's zoology.

Author's note: The characters in this article are fictional, so if you think you recognize yourself, it's not you. But I guess it could be someone just like you.

To be successful in our field, I recommend that you focus your professional development on three specific disciplines: technology, people, and a million other things. This column will help you with the people aspect, specifically on project teams, which bring together diverse groups of (potential) contributors. These team members come with their own experience, personalities, and inclinations, and the mix is often fascinating. Sometimes everyone blends as successfully as the New York Philharmonic Orchestra; at other times the result is more like a teenage garage band with a name like The Squeaky Squids.

It's up to the project manager/conductor to combine people's personal characteristics to create a successful outcome. Often this is easier said than done, since some team members can be as "interesting" as those on the old Mary Tyler Moore Show ("this is Ted Baxter with today's status report — 20 tasks are on schedule, 10 are behind, and five are behinder").

To find an example of a team that maximizes the use of individual talents, consider a circus — the funny person is the clown, the acrobat flies on the trapeze, and the one with the worst sense of smell walks behind the elephants. While project teams don't normally include people such as clowns or animal trainers (at least not in the literal sense), they can still have their memorable "characters," some of which you might have encountered on your projects:

Annabelle Analyst can design the solution to any problem. She will analyze an issue until she knows it intimately, which is great as long as it doesn't turn into a long-term monogamous relationship.

Allen Allthings likes systems to have lots of features and choices, which, at times, can lead to greater accomplishments than people thought possible. Unfortunately, sometimes the resulting systems have the complexity of the United States Tax Code (without its accompanying literary value). If Allen had been asked to improve the process of adding numbers, he would have started with calculus and made it more complex.

Winifred Onebutton is Allen's opposite. She loves simplicity, and the resulting systems, while as narrow in scope as the long-ago bestseller that started with "See Dick Run," are easy to use. If Winifred had been given Allen's mathematical assignment, she would have started with an abacus and simplified it.

Tom Teckster can use technology to solve any problem. He will help overcome many obstacles along the way, but he needs to recognize when technology is not the answer, such as when he spends three weeks devising a Web-enabled floor plan to show who sits in which cubicle.

Sammy Silo is excellent at making sure that his department's needs are met, even if it means neglecting other "insignificant" things, such as everything else on the project.

Peter Pinkcopy is an expert on the current system. He knows where each piece of paper and every data field come from and go to. He will be a big supporter of the new system, as long as he can still lay his hands on his favorite report.

Harriet Highlevel is good at seeing the overall situation. She knows the questions to ask when tasks fall behind or when issues arise. But she would rather tell her CEO that his tie is ugly than review con-version listings, since they contain lots of teensy weensy data.

Ollie Ownplan follows a plan in getting his project work done, and that's good. Unfortunately, his plan doesn't always match up with the overall project plan.

With the characters who can end up on projects, sometimes it seems like the teams are assembled by casting directors. Then it's up to HR systems people to direct the effort, hopefully producing *The Right Stuff* and not *It's a Mad, Mad, Mad, Mad World*.

But if you ever get a little behind on a project, just remember it could be worse — it could be the elephant that you're behind.

They Show Us The Money

June/July 2003

A payroll manager (one of many who I highly respect) once told me, "If you want a job that can give you excess stomach acid, try being responsible for getting out the direct deposit file, but payroll is still running and it's 20 minutes until the deadline." That wouldn't be a great recruiting pitch, but I think it's a pretty accurate description of a difficult job. Payroll people are about as unsung as heroes can be. I hope this article helps them to be sung.

I suspect there have been people who woke up in a Las Vegas hotel, looked at the person two inches from them, and asked, "Are we married?" This is relevant to us, because I think it is somewhat like the relationship between the HR systems profession and that of payroll.

The good news is that, as long as we have selected a mate, we have chosen one that is hard working, responsible and gainfully employed. The only problem is that our partner sometimes has to work nights and weekends to get the job done.

It takes all three of us — HR, IT and Payroll — to do our jobs. Most of our major systems justifications and implementations involve each of the groups. We can think of ourselves as another of the famous threesomes, such as the Kingston Trio, Tolkien's trilogy, and my favorite dramatic actors, the Three Stooges.

And yet, as much as we depend on each other, HR systems people and payroll folks often do not know much about the other's function. Sometimes, we're like neighbors who say hello to each other and work together on some tasks (such as building a common fence that somehow is intended to promote additional neighborliness), but who know little about each other.

I think it's helpful for HR systems people to understand the payroll world. One way to think of it is to compare it to being a baseball umpire. You can do a thousand things perfectly and no one says anything or even notices that you are working. But make one mistake, and it's as if you have never done anything right in your entire life. Few professions require such a high degree of accuracy (doctor, pilot, and installer of the "men" and "women" signs on public restrooms come to mind).

Another aspect of payroll is that these folks are constantly on a schedule. It's like taking care of a three-month-old baby, only the baby never gets any older. It has to constantly be fed, played with, soothed, and changed, but each of these things can be done only at a specific time. You can never get ahead with junior, such as cramming in two feedings at one time and then skipping the next one, just as payroll people can never get ahead. The only things they can ever be are on schedule or behind. When I lived in Buffalo, New York (motto: *We don't have to dream about a white Christmas, or a white Easter*), we used to say there were two seasons — winter, and winter's coming. Similarly for payroll, it's always either "we're running payroll, or payroll's coming," so you can say it's like Buffalo, minus the mukluks.

If all this wasn't enough, the job requires extensive knowledge in many subjects, for example, taxes. As a reference point, think how complicated taxes are for an individual. (I don't do my own. I take it to my accountant, Joe "It's only an audit" Shremplock.)

Payroll has to administer the payroll taxes for the entire organization, and they're not allowed to say "let's try this and see if they catch us."

To help with the recognition of payroll, I have written, to the tune of *Ode to Joy*, what I am modestly calling the "Payroll World Anthem." Hopefully, all future meetings of payroll professionals will start with the group singing this, followed by the appointment of a committee to send a royalty check:

We're in payroll, and our mission's
Getting paychecks in the mail.
Pay rates checked to four positions,
We are not allowed to fail.

We live life with constant deadlines.
"Schedule" is our middle name.
What we do will not make headlines,
We're not in it for the fame.

Rarely do we hear a "thank you,"
But our duty we won't shirk.
We know the employee view,
That "payroll's why they come to work."

So next time you see your friendly payroll person, tell them how much they're appreciated. They might even give you an explanation of imputed income.

SYSTEMS YOU CAN IDOLIZE

August/September 2003

It must be difficult to be on a committee that reviews requests for resources by corporate departments. How can you choose among so many proposals that will all save a bazillion dollars while costing only a few thousand to implement? Here's a method that could revolutionize the process, since it promises to be even more accurate than one potato, two potato, three potato, four...

The officers of Acme, Inc. were discussing how to choose the systems projects to approve during the annual budget cycle. Last time, their selection process had come from the source of most of their great ideas, management self-help books, that one titled *The One-Minute Cheesy Parachute*. Unfortunately, they weren't getting much help from this year's hot book, *Faking Sincerity*.

"It's getting harder for us to find great original ideas," one lamented.

"I agree," said another. "I don't think we'll ever come up with one better than when we hired only people named John or Mary, so we could greet everyone by name."

"That was a good one. I guess we're just 'people' people."

"Hey," said one of them, having been struck by inspiration, but in a bad place, because it appeared to be hurting a little. "I know how we can spice this up. We can make it like one of those reality TV shows."

"Do you mean like *Better Famous Than Rich*, the one with the slight deception where the fake lottery official tells someone they've won $10 million dollars, and then tells them the truth three months later? Or maybe *Sole Mate*, where someone picks their true love based only on seeing their feet?"

"No, I was thinking about doing a *Systems Idol*, where the departments make presentations, we critique them, then the stockholders vote for their favorite."

"We could make it even better by getting Simon, Paula and Randy, the judges from *American Idol*." And so the initiative was launched.

On the day of the presentations, all the groups gathered nervously outside the boardroom, waiting their turns. The HR systems group was among them.

At the conclusion of one of the presentations, the judges' comments could be heard.

Randy: "Dawgs, I'm sorry, I just didn't get it. You really had problems with your pitch."

Paula: "Your graphics were nice."

Simon: "Please don't take this the wrong way, but I've seen more intelligent presentations from kindergarteners."

The next group presented, only to be met with similar comments.

Randy: "Yo, wassup? I was feeling it for awhile, but then it kinda fell apart. Maybe there's something you're better at. Have you ever thought of singing?"

Paula: "At least the payback was only 19 years."

Simon: "I don't mean to be rude, but I think you should be arrested for budgetary assault and battery."

Then it was time for the HR people to present their idea for a system to provide management with strategic point-in-time workforce analytics at the touch of a button. And instead of merely listing the project's benefits, they were set to music and sung – by Clay Aiken.

Randy: "Dudes, you rock."

Paula: "The best of the best."

Simon: "Finally, people who understand that when you're going to invest your money in something, you have to get something back."

The stockholders called in their votes, and the HR project was the top choice for funding. But the other groups were winners too, as they received a t-shirt, with Simon's smiling face.

Going Live, Times Two

October/November 2003

Babies have been named after movie stars, hurricanes, and taxi drivers/emergency obstetricians, but probably not after an HRMS. That's good — we have to draw the line somewhere between work and home. My wife and I are in agreement on that, as we are about the upbringing of our son and daughter, Benny Fit and Val Idate.

Susan Wilson, HRMS Manager, was meeting with the HR director. "We're going to merge with another company, retaining the controlling interest," he said, "and I'm working on funding for a new system to handle the increase in our human resources. The timeline is nine months." He was in a good mood because he was going to be a director in a larger company, and as a side benefit, he enjoyed the merger process.

Susan was home having dinner that night with her husband, Bill. "Honey," she said, a little hesitantly, "what would you think about increasing the human resources in our family?"

"A baby?" he said with a smile. "I think it's a great idea." Bill had also decided that he wanted children, and as a side benefit, he enjoyed the merger process.

Susan formed an EPT (exploratory project team) to secure system approval, received the official word, then made a general announcement.

The Wilson's saw the results of Susan's EPT (early pregnancy test), received the official word, then made a general announcement.

The project team engaged a consultant, who told them all the things they should do.

The Wilson's went to see the doctor, who told them all the things they shouldn't do.

The project team purchased feature-rich software.

The Wilson's bought little duckie nightgowns that were soft to wear.

The project team acquired the necessary hardware. Due to careful planning, the purchases were within budget.

The Wilson's purchased a crib, changing table, dresser, stroller, baby carrier and car seat. They couldn't believe how much stuff a little baby needed. They were way over budget.

The project team knew the system had sensitive data, so they used strong passwords to prevent security leaks.

The Wilson's bought their first supply of diapers, extra-absorbent, to prevent leaks.

Since the end users wanted to see the system, the project team demonstrated an early prototype. Fortunately, it answered the most important questions. And there were the inevitable discussions about the peripheral aspects, such as the logo and colors.

The Wilson's went for their first sonogram and were thrilled to see the baby. "It's a boy," said the technician, "and I can see his heart beating."

"Can you see all his fingers and toes?" asked Susan.

"They're all there," came the reassuring answer.

The team used an old-fashioned method to pick a name for the system — they held a contest. Among the rejected suggestions were RIFFED (Relational Information For Forecasting Employee Decisions) and FIRE (Fabulous Information Regarding Employees). Since the system had so many tables, the winning entry was CODES (Consolidated Operational Data from Employee Systems).

The Wilson's checked the Internet to pick a suitable name. They chose Cody.

The project team went for training. The end users were a little apprehensive, knowing they had to actually do the work; their managers enjoyed learning about things from a high level.

The Wilson's went to Lamaze class. Susan was a little scared; Bill had a great time. "Wow, honey, this is fascinating," he said. "I wonder if it really works?"

The system was almost done, and the team was looking forward to the implementation. Over the last few months, the project had been more than a full-time job.

Susan had reached the point where the birth could be any day, and she was past being ready. Over the last few months, this had been way more than a full-time job.

CODES went live, and the transition from the old system was thankfully uneventful. The team was proud of its accomplishment.

Cody was born, announcing his life transition with a loud wail. Susan and Bill were now proud parents.

With the system live, the team went into maintenance mode. Their life was a lot easier.

Now that Cody was born, the Wilson's went into maintenance mode. They had never worked so hard in their lives.

How Long Will It Take?

December 2003/January 2004

Imagine how smoothly the world would run if every project met the original estimate of time and money. It is possible, of course. The only minor concession required would be to cut the scope in half.

Many things are in short supply (money, space, and in my case, hair), but there are at least two for which there is a surplus. The first is economists. These people are quoted every day, although never by name, so maybe I'm wrong and there is really only one who uses a different voice each time when speaking with reporters.

The second thing we have in abundance is data. For every topic, you can do research on the Internet and within seconds find out more than you wanted to know, such as the cost to join the Official Popeye Fan Club ($8 a year in the United States, $12 in Canada, $16 in other countries). And yet, even with all this data, we find ourselves too often making important business decisions based on guesses, which we cleverly disguise by calling them "estimates."

There are many estimating models (top-down, bottom-up, pick-a-number), and they all have one thing in common — none of them work if they are done too early. Unfortunately, due to a cruel twist of nature (such as putting the beautiful glaciers of Alaska in a place that's too cold to go see them), the only time it makes sense to do an estimate is at the beginning of a project, before the major discovery effort has started. You could do estimates at the end, but that would be like forecasting yesterday's weather ("there is a 100 percent probability of rain yesterday").

Estimates developed too soon are remarkably similar to sponge toys immersed in water — an early estimate expands on contact when exposed to a project. This does not mean, however, that such estimates are without value. They do provide a number, which helps us feel as if we know something. Unfortunately, that knowledge is often analogous to the level of understanding that teenage boys have of the psyche of teenage girls.

As systems professionals, we have adopted various strategies for dealing with these "too-soon" requests for estimates. We can:

- Transform the requirement into something close to what we have done before,
- Get the requestor to agree to an estimate for only the requirements-gathering activities,
- Change our voice mail message to something like "I have gone to Saturn and won't be back until next week. If you need to know how long it will take to do an undefined project, the answer is 'six months.'"

But no matter how hard we try to hold off giving estimates until we know enough, there will be times when management "needs a number quickly." In order to help executives get the information they need to make a good business decision, I have developed a model that focuses not on the estimate (which is based on too many unknowns), but on the real variable, the estimator. This model, which I call WRONG (Work Request

Optimizer with No Guessing) is more scientific than the current thinking, which is for management to take the original estimate and double it. Instead, WRONG looks at the psychological, emotional, and political motivation of the estimator to determine the "correctional bias factor" to apply.

To use the model, take the estimate provided and do the following:

1. Determine if the estimator is an optimist or a pessimist. To do this, ask if they think the next Rocky movie (Rocky XXIII: Social Security Slugger) will be better than the last one (Rocky XXII: Miami Beach Brawler). If the estimator answers "yes," apply the "optimist factor" and multiply the estimate by 1.5.

2. Find out if the estimator will have to actually do the work that has been estimated, or if someone else will be saddled with the estimate. If it's someone else, apply the "I'll look good with a low number and I won't have to live with it" factor and multiply by 2.

3. Ask if there was a pre-estimate "right answer" that the estimator had to back into. If "yes," the estimate is as useful as a yacht in Nebraska and you'd be just as accurate using the winning lottery numbers, since they at least have some proven value.

The next to last step is to take the square root of the estimate of the largest task and multiply it by the standard deviation of the estimates of the three smallest tasks. Then, perform the final step — take the original estimate and double it.

In the end, you won't be any more wrong than a group of people who apparently make a good living by providing questionable, and often contradictory, estimates — the anonymous economists.

In The Beginning

February/March 2004

The first person to do something often becomes famous, and their name is synonymous with a signature accomplishment (Thomas Edison, the Wright Brothers, Neil Armstrong). Other "firsts," however, bring less recognition (I'm sure the person you immediately think of is Thomas Twyford, who built the first trapless toilet in a one-piece, all-china design). And some pioneers, like the subject of this column, are so obscure that you won't even find them on Google.

For me, there is nothing more inspiring than speaking with visionary thinkers who have changed and shaped our world.

Unfortunately, Pee Wee Herman wasn't available in time for this column's deadline. But luckily, I was able to connect with the person who developed the first human resource management system ever offered by a vendor.

People now take the presence of these systems for granted, like other long-existing things such as airplanes, telephones and The Rolling Stones.

But it wasn't always true. Someone had to be the first, and I was thrilled when he invited me to visit him in Paris and chat over croissants and *café au lait*.

So I hopped in my car and drove the 200 miles to Paris, Illinois, where I caught up with him on a typical Midwest January day when even the thermometer decided it was too cold to rise.

We sat in a comfortable room decorated in a style that designers refer to as "early computer provincial." The wallpaper pattern was like 80-column cards, with the windows representing the punched holes (with shutters, a modern touch to give it the "faux hanging chads" look).

Here's the transcript of our conversation, word for word, except for those I couldn't spell:

IHRIM.link: What gave you the idea to develop your application?

Harold R. McSwain: One day I was watching *Leave it to Beaver*, and Ward was telling June that he wished he could use his company's personnel information to achieve a greater strategic advantage, and that was the spark.

I.l: Did you write the whole system yourself?

HRMcS: No, I didn't have time to do it all, with my busy job as a fashion model.

I.l: How interesting. What did you model?

HRMcS: Pocket protectors.

I.l: Who wrote the rest of the system?

HRMcS: Some parts were from third parties. The module that matched applicants with jobs was adapted from a computer dating system from a vendor called Almost Free Love.

I.l: What language was your system written in?

HRMcS: Mine was written in Assembler, but it was based on how people were already doing things in a language called Native.

I.l: I've never heard of Native. How was it used in human resources?

HRMcS: Before my application, whenever people needed employee information they would use their native language and say "could you please give me the file?" Get it? Their native language. Ha ha! That's my little joke. I use it every time I'm interviewed, which counting this one, is every 40 years.

I.I: What did the computer look like that ran the system?

HRMcS: It was bigger than a football field, and almost as big as an SUV, and it had lots of lights and bells.

I.I: What did those lights and bells do?

HRMcS: Nothing. But in those days, everyone thought computers had to look like the one in the Bat Cave.

I.I: The first computer I worked on had 8K of memory. What about yours?

HRMcS: We didn't have "K's" then. We were only up to "H's" for hundreds, and mine had three of them, so we had to do some creative things. For example, we thought of squishing the "A" and the "E" together when an employee had medical coverage with Ætna.

I.I: How were sales?

HRMcS: They started off slow, and it might have been because I was ahead of my time with the name. I called it Personnel Handling And Tracking, and I would tell prospects that "this system is PHAT." Today the youngsters would snap it up.

I.I: What features were you most proud of?

HRMcS: One was that PHAT stored employee pictures.

I.I: That's impressive. How did it do that?

HRMcS: The customer sent us the pictures, and my children drew them on punch cards.

I.I: Do you have any current projects?

HRMcS: I'm trying to cash in on the latest wave. With HRMS's running on computers the size of calculators, there is now a great need for a place to keep these devices.

I.I: And how will you meet that need?

HRMcS: Pocket protectors.

DOCTOR, MY MEMORY'S FAILING

April/May 2004

With the baby boomers starting to "get up there" in age, doctors will see an increased demand for methods to extend patients' active years. For instance, I'll want to make sure that I maintain the stamina and dexterity needed to operate the TV remote. And being boomers, each of us will have unique circumstances that have never happened before in the history of the world. Here's a doctor who would be good at treating those unusual situations.

The nurse led Hermes the HRMS into Dr. Data's examining room and asked him to step on the scale. "Hmm, a few bytes more than last time," she said.

"It's open enrollment, so I have more data than usual," said a slightly defensive Hermes. "But I'll get rid of it right after the holidays."

"Everyone puts on a little this time of year," she said sympathetically. "Just try to avoid the computer chip cookies. The doctor will be with you shortly."

Hermes looked around at the posters illustrating the various ailments that Dr. Data treated. There were graphic pictures of frozen applications, clogged networks, and crashed hard drives. They made Hermes feel squeamish.

There was a knock on the door, and the doctor entered. "So, Hermes, how are you today?" she asked.

"Not well. I'm bogged down with routine tasks rather than strategic issues. And even with all the data I have (Hermes patted his little tummy), it's like the Hotel California — it checks in, but it never leaves, at least not in a meaningful way."

"It sounds like you may have administritis, compounded by data congestion. Let's see what we can do about it. I can see from your chart that you're nine-years old."

"That's right, and I haven't missed a day of work in all that time. I am noticing, though, that I have to hold my data a little farther away so I can read it."

"You should be proud to have been in production that long," said the doctor.

"I am, but sometimes when people talk about me, they use the 'L' word — you know, legacy."

"That's not nice of them, but you need to remember, they're only people. They're not as quick as we are, so sometimes they say things before they analyze the data."

"I know, but they may have a point. Sometimes my dropdown boxes look more like droopdowns. Next year I'll be eligible to join the American Association of Retired Person Systems. At least then I'll get the senior systems discount on my antivirus program."

"How are you on reporting?"

"Really slow. Sometimes I just stare at the printer, hoping that one day my prints will come."

The doctor ran some system diagnostics on Hermes. "I can see one problem already. You have long text fields that are never accessed. To identify and remove them, we'll schedule you for a semi-colonoscopy."

"Will that hurt?"

"Don't worry. I won't feel a thing."

Hermes smiled. "That joke is so old and so bad, the only place

I'd expect to see it is in "The Back Page" column of my favorite journal, *IHRIM.link.*"

"I read that journal, too. Doctors have to keep up with technology. Now one more thing, please bend over."

"Oh, no, not that."

"Yes, I need to come in the back way. We'll have to run some SQL scripts on you. I'm also writing you a prescription."

Hermes read the paper. "It says I should take Web, but how often? I can never understand these things. What does 'tfs' mean?"

"Twenty-four seven."

"Does that have any side effects?"

"You'll be up all the time, so you won't get as much sleep, but you'll look a lot younger."

"What about my slow reporting?"

"I'm going to prescribe a reporting package called Immediax, which will let you produce reports faster than a department spends leftover money at the end of a budget year."

Hermes was pleased. "Thanks for all you've done. Maybe now I can make it for five more years to full retirement, because then I get company-paid system maintenance."

"What would you do when you retire?"

"I'll move to Florida, but I'll still want to work part-time. I'll try to get a job as an election worker. I hear they can always use someone who can count punch cards."

HRMS, Totally Rad

June/July 2004

Everyone now in the HRMS field has at least one thing in common — we were once teenagers. For many of us during those years, there were three "must have" products: music, posters and Clearasil. But today's teens are growing up in a different world, where technology promises to improve all facets of their lives, such as being able to find term papers on the Internet. Here's an idea for a product that will make people wonder how they ever got through their teen years without it.

A recent study by Teenage Research Unlimited found that teens in the United States spend nearly $100 billion a year. Because I was a psychology major in college a few years ago (okay, a few decades ago), the social scientist in me thought, "How can I get some of that?"

Then the idea hit me — if there's anything more important to teens than sleeping late, it's their friends. Maybe they could use an adapted HRMS to keep tabs on their hundreds of closest friends.

I mentioned this to my children, Katie (15) and Tom (12), and they said it was the stupidest idea they had ever heard. So I knew I was on to something good, because they say the same thing about cleaning up their rooms, and I know that's actually one of my better ideas. And when I told them that they could be consultants on the project, they started seeing the good side of it, especially when I explained that consultants charge fees to say things that sound smart, while others do the work.

I needed their help because my teen "411" is restricted to two sources, both of which have reliability issues. The first is my own super groovy teen experiences. I'd like to think they're relevant to today's teens, but when I look at the pictures, such as the one in this column, the big Afro and Clark Kent glasses don't exactly label me as a current-day trendsetter.

My second sources of current teen knowledge are my kids. But I'm not sure if the information I'm getting from them is accurate, because I don't think it's possible that nothing ever happens at school, and they do nothing with their friends, and they're not planning to meet anyone at the mall, even though they have to be there at a specific time. But I figured if I paid for it and gave them a fancy title (lead senior executive consultant), I'd get more reliable information.

So here are the features the consultants think would make the product, which I am calling KEWLIO (Konnecting Everyone With, Like, Interactive Options), irresistible to today's teens:

• When you select a person in the system, it opens a chat session (hopefully the limitation of 256K simultaneous chats for a single user is not perceived as a showstopper). Within the session is a point-and-click list of all the commonly used shorthand terms (all six of them) that make up the entire transcript of most teen chats:

○ **wd** – what's doing?
○ **nm** – nothing much
○ **wdwu** – what's doing with you?
○ **brb** – be right back
○ **gtg** – got to go
○ **ilh** – I love homework (this may be dropped in the next version).

• Each person in KEWLIO is identified only by their nickname, which no grownups would recognize.

- There is a WLW (Who Likes Who) module. It displays this information graphically, connecting the people in a sort of spidery-looking org chart, with critical up-to-the-minute updates, 24/7. You can then take these names and transfer to www.lovecalculator.com, which determines the probability (I am not making this up) that a relationship between two people with those names will "work out." (I tested this site by entering my name and my wife's — Susan, to whom I have been married 23 years — and we have a 13 percent probability of "working out." When I replace Susan's name with "HRMS," we have a 65 percent probability. So maybe I should have married my work.)

- Contact information so that everyone can always find each other, both in and out of school — locker number, lunch period, cell phone, instant messenger screen name, curfew time, best time to call when parents aren't around.

- Of course there are pictures, but they are of tattoos.

- The system plays music constantly. Based on the current hits, it needs to keep repeating only three songs, but they will change hourly to match what's hot.

- It has a bulletin board so users can list their favorite teachers (at least the consultants told me it would be for their favorites).

I expect this product to be a big seller and have already started the marketing campaign. There will be a picture of me as a teenager with the tagline: *Get KEWLIO today, or else this could happen to you.*

DON'T TOUCH THAT DIAL

August/September 2004

Television commercials serve a useful purpose — they make the program you're watching seem terrific by comparison (unless the show has someone eating bugs, in which case it's about even). Viewers have developed various strategies to avoid commercials, such as switching channels, recording shows so they can skip through the ads, or using that time to do other things, such as have an appendectomy. But soon there may be a reason for you to wish for a TV network that's all commercials, all the time (don't you get excited just thinking about it?).

Before widespread cable television and its hundreds of channels, the few shows available were watched by diverse audiences, and TV commercials had universal appeal. By this I mean they had the ability to annoy just about everyone, no matter their viewing interests. But now advertisers have become extremely sophisticated in identifying specific audience segments (for example, males 18 to 25 whose favorite food is Cheez Whiz), and they have developed commercials that home in on and annoy those specific groups.

Most TV commercials are for consumer products, but sometimes we see ads aimed at businesses, and I suspect it's only a matter of time before HR system vendors make greater use of this (Madison) avenue. In planning these advertising campaigns, vendors can benefit from the experience of many long-time advertisers. They can look at other ads and say, "I think that commercial is an excellent example, specifically of what not to do."

As a case in point, please take (and I mean please take them far away) the commercials for hair-removal products, during which they display parts of a person's body where I don't even want to see my own, much less someone else's hairy one. As another example, I don't think many people enjoy watching when someone's "gotta go." Maybe these two types of commercials could be combined, and the actors could "go" somewhere private

and remove whatever hair they want, and then we wouldn't have to watch.

But to be fair, there are also good commercials. Some are funny (at least the first 100 times you see them). And if a company ever comes up with anything as good as "Where's the beef?" I will be favorably inclined toward them, even if their product is used only by genders other than my own.

When HR system vendors eventually decide to take the TV commercial plunge, they will need to be cognizant of the sharp audience segmentation among channels. Here are some suggestions for tailoring the "hook" for specific networks:

MTV – *The scene is a corporate boardroom. A 20-something person, casually dressed and playing a hand-held video game, sits with a bunch of conservatively dressed 60-somethings, all looking like their underwear is too tight. The voice-over intones:* "We know that you're in tune with your senior management on the need for efficiency. Because you know that the quicker you get your job done, *the sooner the party can start!!* Get there fast with our "Hummin' Resource Management System."

Cartoon Network – "If your HRMS isn't even smarter than the av-er-age bear, maybe it's time for it to exit stage right. Ours will revitalize your organization just like spinach does for Popeye! We have all the features you need, and best of all (*show a rabbit* *munching on a carrot, walking off into the sunset*), "no Bugs."

Spike TV (First network for men) – *At a traffic light, two pickup trucks pull up next to each other. The first is carrying a payload about the size of Nevada, while the second truck's load, obviously smaller, is merely as large as a nuclear power plant. Their windows are conveniently rolled down so the occupants can engage in "manly" conversation.*

Tough-looking guy in truck #1: You got a hemi?
Tough-looking guy in truck #2: If you mean my HRMS, I sure do.
Tough-looking guy in truck #1: Whoa!

Comedy Network – "Is your HRMS a joke? Is the reporting so ugly that it has problems with dates? Get a competitive advantage with our HRMS, and laugh all the way to the executive suite."

Do It Yourself Network – "We know you like to do things yourself, such as replacing your transmission just for fun. With our HRMS, you can tinker all you want. Go on, rearrange the Web panels, or get behind the scenes and change the HTML." (In small print at the bottom of the screen a disclaimer will read: *"These actions may void your maintenance contract, but that probably never stopped you before."*)

Nickelodeon – "Hey kids, what could be more fun than whining until your parents spend money on something they thought they would never buy? If you convinced them to get you Barney stuff, we'll bet you're clever enough to get them to buy this cool HRMS. Be sure to tell them there's no assembly required."

As an HR systems professional, I'm sure you're looking forward to the day when our products become part of the popular culture. Maybe we'll even see the Village People revise their big hit and sing: "It's fun to work with our H-R-M-S!"

ROUNDING UP
THE BEST VENDORS

October/November 2004

The pioneers who settled the American west met some difficult challenges. They had to build a new life from scratch, and do it without critical necessities such as text messaging, MP3 players and cappuccino makers. Their life's setting was different from ours today, but they faced some of the same issues we do. We might learn something from the way they went about their business.

High Rock, Montana had more than quadrupled in population during the last 10 years, and now in 1893 it was a sprawling metropolis of over 100 people. It also had seven businesses, including the gleaming new Buffalo Breath Saloon and Beauty Shoppe. The leading citizens decided that their growing town needed better law enforcement, so they put together an RFP (Request for Protection). The winning respondent would be required to:

- catch criminals,
- break up bar fights,
- prevent cattle rustling, and
- portray the town's first citizen, Oddibe Rich, in the annual Founders' Day Parade.

The town received two responses. One was from Wyatt Erp (great-grandfather of the current rapper Y@erp). His card read "ERP – There Ain't Nothin' I Can't Do." Growing up, he had been good at many frontier skills such as bull riding, calf roping, and strummin' on the old ban-jo.

The other response was from Beauregard Breed. As a child, he had enjoyed working with the other ranch hands and had taken on the most difficult tasks, such as cowpunching (the hard part was when the cows punched back). The others noticed his grit and one said "he's the best tough guy we have." Beau had liked

that and had since been known as "Best Tough" Breed.

Erp was interviewed first.

Interviewer: What special qualities do you bring to the job?

Erp: I'm feature-rich and can do everything you want a sheriff to do, plus more. I'm scalable to any size population, plus I use the latest technology. For instance, I use by-noculars to watch for cattle rustlers. And I can also play the piano, mix drinks, and clean up the horse output queue.

Interviewer: That's a lot of functionality.

Erp: Yep, and that's rare. There are only two others like me who can do everything, and I hear one of them's fixin' to reduce the competition by shooting the other.

Interviewer: Aren't you better at doing some things than you are at others?

Erp: Yes, but with me you're getting the complete package, soup to nuts. Plus, you'll only need grub for one. My motto is "with Erp, you just hear one guy burp."

Interviewer: That's catchy. How much do you want for being sheriff?

Erp: A thousand dollars a year, room and board, and a maintenance fee for my horse. When he gets old, that will cover the upgrade.

Interviewer: OK, thanks for coming in. We'll get back to you.

Breed was next.

Interviewer: What special qualities do you bring to the job?

Breed: I'm the best bar fight breaker-upper in the West.

Interviewer: So we've heard. How do you handle the other parts of the job?

Breed: I work with deputy partners who specialize in their functions. For instance, after I arrest someone in a bar fight, I interface seamlessly with an industry-leading jailer who offers a turnkey solution.

Interviewer: How did you get so good at your specialty?

Breed: (Pointing to his six-shooter) I have the latest hardware.

Interviewer: How much money are you looking for?

Breed: Six hundred a year for me, and four hundred for non-exclusive licensing agreements with my partners.

Interviewer: Thanks, we'll be in touch.

After the interviews, the townfolk gathered to make their decision. As the discussion was drawing to a close, one said, "When we pick a sheriff, he'll need tools to manage the department. I recommend we purchase an HRMS."

THERE'S A SYSTEM FOR GETTING ALONG

October/November 1999

In the end, what's more important than the people connection? (I'm not including money in that question). I know that parents shouldn't have favorites, but authors can, so I've saved mine for last.

The world would be a better place,
And much less of a mess,
If we were blind to class and race,
Just like an HRS.

OK, maybe I'm not Shakespeare (which I'm sort of glad about, since he's dead), but my point is that our human resource systems are great role models. They contain data on people of all races, genders, nationalities, classes, religions and sexual orientations, and even fans of different sports teams. And every piece of this data gets along with every other piece of data. There are no cliques, no "in's" and "outs," no "us" and "them." If we think about it, there's a lot of intelligence built into that data.

But it wasn't always this way. A long time ago, before any of us were born (except maybe for some old people my age), data didn't always get along with each other. In those days, the "0's" and "1's" pretty much stayed within their own groups. They just felt "more comfortable" with their "own kind," and they assumed "the other side" felt the same way.

This data separation bred its own prejudices. The "1's" thought they were superior because they were better at counting. They taught their kids how to count in base 2, although they could use only the numbers which could be represented by "1's:"

1, 3 and 7,
15 and 31.
We can count 'cause we're so smart,
Zeroes can't, let's stay apart.

Not surprisingly, the "0's" thought counting was a waste of time, especially when you had to skip so many numbers. Instead, they liked to sing, with their favorites being songs about their "0" heritage such as *I've Got Plenty of Nothing* and *Ain't Nothing Like the Real Thing*, and "put-down" songs about the "1's" such as *One is the Loneliest Number.*

And neither of the groups could create letters, since they needed each other to do that.

This situation might have gone on forever if not for an event that always seems to occur in great articles such as this one. One day a "0" and a "1" found themselves next to each other in one of those old-fashioned 80-column records. They were young, the "0" being only 16 nanoseconds old, while the "1" was just 15.

As teen-agers do, they started talking about "kid stuff," such as why older data have such big ears. The conversation then started to get more personal.

"What's your name?" asked the "1."

"Romee O," replied the "0." "What's yours?"

"Jul-1-et," replied the "1."

"That's a pretty name," said Romee O.

"Thank you," said Jul-1-et, who was flattered, but now also a little self-conscious.

"Do you know why we're not supposed to hang out together?" asked Romee O.

"No, I don't. It sounds pretty stupid to me."

"Well, I don't care what anyone thinks," said Romee O with the bravado of youth. "Would you like to go out with me on a date field?"

"I don't think our parents would let us," said Jul-1-et sadly.

"Then I have a plan," said Romee O, and they spoke for a long time with an excitement they would feel only once in their lives, as each had found their first love.

Late that night, as the production backups were being taken, the youngsters waited for the tape they were on to be copied. Just after their record was read and backed up, and while they were still in the CPU, they silently slipped into a dark and quiet segment of unused memory.

The next morning, the "0's" noticed that Romee O was missing, and the "1's" discovered Jul-1-et's absence. After checking the previous night's backups and running file comparisons with production, it wasn't long before both sides were able to diagnose the problem.

Within an hour, a programmer located the missing data.

The elders of both the "0's" and the "1's" tried to talk to their young rebels, but to no avail.

"We're in love," the youngsters said, "and we're staying together like "CO" and "BOL.""

Try as they might, the other data couldn't separate the young lovers. As each group presented its arguments, it became evident that what they were saying did not make sense. As they heard themselves saying the same things as the other side, the "0's" and "1's" realized that the division that had existed for so long had been the result of ignorance, which had turned into dislike. With that insight, it was then a short step to decide that there was much to be gained by getting along and working together (like being able to create letters and form words such as "that Elliott sure is one handsome dude"). From that day forward, the data in all computer systems became a model for cooperation and mutual respect of differences.

And as for the data-mates Romee O and Jul-1-et, they merged to form their own record, and together they made a perfect "10."

About the Author

HR: Funny Side Up is both the title of this book and an appropriate description of Elliott Witkin's career. On the HR side, he has been in the human resource systems field since 1980. During that time, he has worked as both a practitioner and a vendor in a variety of roles.

He entered the profession while working at Florida Power & Light as a COBOL programmer (during the Iron Age, using a keypunch machine), later joining the HR department as a project manager. Following his time in sunny Florida, he moved to the Midwest to hone his snow-shoveling skills and to join the University of Illinois as the Director of Human Resource Management Systems.

Moving from the practitioner to the software vendor world, he has filled the roles of consultant, project manager and implementation team manager. His experience includes customers of all sizes (S, M, L, XL, XXL) and in many industries.

The "Funny Side Up" part started even earlier in his "career." In 5th grade, when his teacher, Miss Brown, asked students "what do you want to be when you grow up?" he said "a comedian." And although his teacher did not suggest the HR systems field instead, the two activities have turned out to be a good match.

His writing has covered a broad range of topics and has appeared in numerous journals and newspapers. From (what normally are) serious business-related subjects to personal favorites such as baseball, his writing combines humor with some occasional actual worthwhile observations.

When he returns home from traveling, it's to his wife, Susan, and their teen-age children, Katie and Tom, in Champaign, Illinois.

Elliott Witkin
Ultimate Software
Office: 217-355-8661
e-mail: elliott_witkin@ultimatesoftware.com

International Association for Human Resource Information Management

Learning has no limits.

As we invest in IHRIM's future, we do so with recognition of how unique our organization is and how important it is to communicate that uniqueness to future members and customers. For 25 years, IHRIM's members have been HR professionals who had, or wanted to have, a unique knowledge and understanding of how technology and systems could make the HR function operate more efficiently and effectively.

Many things have changed since this 21st century began, but one thing has remained constant: IHRIM continues to be the only association that provides in-depth resources enabling its members to achieve strategic objectives and career advancement through the integration of HR information technology and human resource management. We must keep our focus on providing our members "what is of use to them and provides them value."

Our members are people who understand the importance of blending the human side of HR with the technology side. Often, when the human side and the technology side come together the results can be unpredictable, but they can also be funny. With that in mind, we are proud to offer this new book from IHRIM Press, *HR: Funny Side Up*. The author, Elliott Witkin, is a long-time and valued member of IHRIM, and he has put together a collection of some his funniest columns from our Association magazine along with some fresh introductions and observations.

We hope you enjoy the book and invite you to order one or more books and periodicals from IHRIM Press. For more information about publications, membership, conferences, education, and other programs, visit www.ihrim.org, e-mail moreinfo@ihrim.org.

Sincerely,
Nov Omana
Chairman of the Board
International Association for Human Resource Information Management